Becomi Assertive Teacher

Being cooperative, empathetic, and accommodating are great qualities for teachers but can also lead to higher rates of frustration and eventually burnout. In this empowering new book from Brad Johnson and Jeremy Johnson, find out how becoming more assertive can help highly agreeable teachers thrive.

First, take personality quizzes to find out how agreeable or assertive you are! Then the authors delve into why that matters. You'll find out how assertiveness differs from aggression and passivity and why it is a valuable tool for teachers, so you can stand up for your own needs and rights while respecting the needs and rights of others. Chapters cover establishing healthy boundaries, learning when to say no, dealing with conflicts, becoming more self-aware, leveraging your strengths, finding your voice, and more!

Each chapter is filled with practical strategies and examples and ends with a toolbox feature to help you build your skills. As you learn to become more assertive, you'll improve your interactions and will feel more heard – and fulfilled – in your teaching role and in life.

Brad Johnson (@DrBradJohnson) has over 25 years of experience as a teacher and administrator at the K–12 and collegiate level. He is author of several books and one of the most inspirational and affirmational speakers in education.

Jeremy Johnson has a master's degree in industrial/organizational psychology, where his research focused on the application of personality theory in the workplace. He has 16 years' experience, including a background in administrative processes and procedure development.

Becoming a More Assertive Teacher

Maximizing Strengths, Establishing Boundaries, and Amplifying Your Voice

Brad Johnson and Jeremy Johnson

Routledge
Taylor & Francis Group

NEW YORK AND LONDON

Designed cover image: © Getty images

First published 2024
by Routledge
605 Third Avenue, New York, NY 10158

and by Routledge
4 Park Square, Milton Park, Abingdon, Oxon, OX14 4RN

Routledge is an imprint of the Taylor & Francis Group, an informa business

© 2024 Brad Johnson and Jeremy Johnson

The right of Brad Johnson and Jeremy Johnson to be identified as authors of this work has been asserted in accordance with sections 77 and 78 of the Copyright, Designs and Patents Act 1988.

Library of Congress Cataloging-in-Publication Data
Names: Johnson, Brad, 1969– author. | Johnson, Jeremy (Psychologist), author.
Title: Becoming a more assertive teacher : maximizing strengths, establishing
    boundaries, and amplifying your voice / Brad Johnson and Jeremy Johnson.
Description: New York, NY : Routledge, 2024.
Identifiers: LCCN 2023033437 (print) | LCCN 2023033438 (ebook) |
    ISBN 9781032592480 (hardback) | ISBN 9781032592176 (paperback) |
    ISBN 9781003453796 (ebook)
Subjects: LCSH: Teachers—Professional relationships. | Teachers—
    Pscyhology. | Assertiveness (Psychology)
Classification: LCC LB1775 .J5449 2024 (print) | LCC LB1775 (ebook) |
    DDC 371.1001/9—dc23/eng/20230831
LC record available at https://lccn.loc.gov/2023033437
LC ebook record available at https://lccn.loc.gov/2023033438

ISBN: 9781032592480 (hbk)
ISBN: 9781032592176 (pbk)
ISBN: 9781003453796 (ebk)

DOI: 10.4324/9781003453796

Typeset in Palatino
by Apex CoVantage, LLC

Contents

8. I believe that it is important to be respectful and considerate of others, even in difficult situations.

1	2	3	4	5
Strongly Disagree	Disagree	Neutral	Agree	Strongly Agree

9. Students and colleagues see me as an empathetic person.

1	2	3	4	5
Strongly Disagree	Disagree	Neutral	Agree	Strongly Agree

10. My presence makes students and colleagues feel at ease.

1	2	3	4	5
Strongly Disagree	Disagree	Neutral	Agree	Strongly Agree

11. I feel genuine concern for students and colleagues.

1	2	3	4	5
Strongly Disagree	Disagree	Neutral	Agree	Strongly Agree

12. Others would consider me soft-hearted.

1	2	3	4	5
Strongly Disagree	Disagree	Neutral	Agree	Strongly Agree

13. I tend to put others before myself.

1	2	3	4	5
Strongly Disagree	Disagree	Neutral	Agree	Strongly Agree

14. I empathize with my student's and colleague's situations.

1	2	3	4	5
Strongly Disagree	Disagree	Neutral	Agree	Strongly Agree

15. I tend to be indirect in dealing with issues with others.

1	2	3	4	5
Strongly Disagree	Disagree	Neutral	Agree	Strongly Agree

Total Score _____

Remember, this is a facet of personality, and no one side of the spectrum is better than another. Certain traits are more effective for certain tasks.

15–29: Based on this score, you may have a low level of agreeableness. This means that you may place a high value on independence, critical thinking, and personal goals.

30–44: Based on this score, you may have a low-medium level of agreeableness. This means that you may place a higher value on independence, critical thinking, and personal goals compared to things like team goals and collaboration. Remember, this is a facet of personality, and no one side of the spectrum is better than another.

45–59: Based on this score, you may have a medium-high level of agreeableness. This means that you may be more likely to be cooperative and a peace-keeper. You may also prefer team-based goals to personal goals.

60–75: This means that you may be highly agreeable. Individuals who are highly agreeable are highly flexible, thrive in teamwork settings, and advocate for others. They may also have difficulty being assertive, take on too much responsibility, and get taken advantage of.

Reflection Quiz 2:

1. I have no issue dealing with difficult situations involving confrontation.

1	2	3	4	5
Strongly Disagree	Disagree	Neutral	Agree	Strongly Agree

2. Talking to people in positions of authority does not make me feel nervous, self-conscious, or unsure of myself.

1	2	3	4	5
Strongly Disagree	Disagree	Neutral	Agree	Strongly Agree

3. I express my opinions, even if others in the group disagree with me.

1	2	3	4	5
Strongly Disagree	Disagree	Neutral	Agree	Strongly Agree

4. I tend to speak often in group settings.

1	2	3	4	5
Strongly Disagree	Disagree	Neutral	Agree	Strongly Agree

5. I always know what I want and how to get it.

1	2	3	4	5
Strongly Disagree	Disagree	Neutral	Agree	Strongly Agree

6. I find it easy to ask the tough questions or present opposing viewpoints to other's ideas.

1	2	3	4	5
Strongly Disagree	Disagree	Neutral	Agree	Strongly Agree

7. I feel comfortable saying no to people.

1	2	3	4	5
Strongly Disagree	Disagree	Neutral	Agree	Strongly Agree

8. I step in and make decisions for others.

1	2	3	4	5
Strongly Disagree	Disagree	Neutral	Agree	Strongly Agree

9. When a situation is unfair, I bring attention to it.

1	2	3	4	5
Strongly Disagree	Disagree	Neutral	Agree	Strongly Agree

10. I speak clearly and address situations directly.

1	2	3	4	5
Strongly Disagree	Disagree	Neutral	Agree	Strongly Agree

11. I have a difficult time compromising my needs, wants, or goals.

1	2	3	4	5
Strongly Disagree	Disagree	Neutral	Agree	Strongly Agree

12. I can get a teammate or a peer to change their behavior if the person disagrees.

1	2	3	4	5
Strongly Disagree	Disagree	Neutral	Agree	Strongly Agree

13. I speak up immediately when someone is not respecting my personal boundaries.

1	2	3	4	5
Strongly Disagree	Disagree	Neutral	Agree	Strongly Agree

14. I can get a person to understand my own ideas even if my ideas are different from theirs.

1	2	3	4	5
Strongly Disagree	Disagree	Neutral	Agree	Strongly Agree

15. I have no problem refusing requests from others.

1	2	3	4	5
Strongly Disagree	Disagree	Neutral	Agree	Strongly Agree

Total Score _____

Remember, this is a facet of personality, and no one side of the spectrum is better than another. Certain traits are more effective for certain tasks.

15–29: Based on a score in this range, you may be low in assertiveness. This means that you may be more reserved and hesitant in expressing your thoughts, feelings, and needs. You may avoid conflict and try to maintain harmony in their relationships, often at the expense of your own desires or interests.

30–44: A score in this range means that you may have a low-moderate level of assertiveness. This suggests that you have the ability to assert yourself to a certain extent or that you have a higher threshold for when you choose to do so. You may feel comfortable expressing your opinions and needs in some situations but not in others. It's possible that you may benefit from developing your assertiveness skills further to communicate more effectively and build stronger relationships with others.

45–59: A score in this range means that you may be medium-high in assertiveness. This means you can be assertive but may not always feel comfortable doing so. You may assert yourself in situations where you feel strongly about the outcome but may also avoid conflict in other situations. It's possible that you may benefit from developing assertiveness skills and learning how to communicate more effectively to achieve your goals and build more fulfilling relationships.

60–75: Based on a score in this range, you may be highly assertive. This means that you are confident and self-assured in expressing your thoughts, feelings, and needs. You are comfortable taking charge of situations and advocating for themselves, even in the face of opposition or challenges. Highly assertive individuals tend to be effective communicators who can clearly and directly articulate their expectations and boundaries to others.

Think of these reflections as your trusted allies, guiding you on your quest to become an even more exceptional educator. They provide a mirror into your teaching journey, allowing you to examine your strengths, areas for improvement, and the impact you have on your students' lives. As you read through the book, let your reflections guide you towards strategies that resonate with your goals and aspirations.

Embrace the power of these dimensions as you embark on your noble quest to educate and inspire future generations. Within these reflections lies the key to unlocking your fullest potential. With each step, you'll grow, adapt, collaborate, and positively influence the lives of your students. Your journey towards growth and impact begins now, dear educator. Embrace the magic of teacher reflections and let your light shine brightly upon the world of education.

1

Understanding the Benefits and Pitfalls of High Agreeableness

Abraham Wald was a Hungarian-Jewish mathematician and statistician who worked on a range of problems during World War II, including the issue of reinforcing planes. In particular, he was tasked with analyzing the damage to U.S. Army Air Force planes that had returned from missions over Europe.

One of the assumptions at the time was that the areas that were most heavily damaged were the areas that needed the most protection. And most of the scientists and engineers decided that these were the areas that most needed to be reinforced.

However, Wald realized that this was a mistake because the planes that had returned were the planes that had survived their missions and thus had not been hit in the most critical areas.

Instead of going along with the other experts just to be agreeable, Wald proposed that the areas that had not been hit were the areas that needed the most protection. He reasoned that the planes that had been shot down were likely to have been hit in critical areas that were not present on the planes that had returned. By focusing on the areas that had not been hit, Wald argued that it was possible to identify the areas that were most critical for the survival of the plane (O'Connor, 2005).

Wald's approach led to the counterintuitive conclusion that the planes did not need more protection in the areas that had been heavily damaged but rather in the areas that had not been

DOI: 10.4324/9781003453796-1

hit at all. This led to the redesign of U.S. Army Air Forces planes with additional protection in critical areas that had previously been overlooked. Because he was willing to risk speaking up instead of just being agreeable, he changed how planes were constructed. As teachers, while it may be our nature to be agreeable, are we missing out on best practices because we aren't willing to speak up?

Positive Traits

As educators, we best relate to the positive aspects of agreeableness because these are the traits through which we build connections with students and help them become their best. People who are high in agreeableness tend to prioritize cooperation, harmony, and tolerance. They are empathetic and compassionate towards others, which allows them to form strong relationships.

One of the key characteristics of agreeableness is empathy. Empathy is the ability to understand and share the feelings of others. You must be able to empathize with their students in order to understand their needs and create a supportive learning environment. This is particularly important for teachers who work with young children who may be experiencing a wide range of emotions.

Another trait associated with agreeableness is nurturing. Nurturing involves caring for others and helping them to develop and grow. You are responsible for nurturing their students' intellectual, emotional, and social growth. This requires a high level of patience, compassion, and dedication.

As a teacher, you must also be cooperative to work effectively with other teachers, school administrators, and parents. It's crucial to be willing to listen, compromise, and collaborate to achieve common goals. Working effectively with your students is equally important for creating a positive learning environment.

Your agreeable nature is a strength in this regard. Your patience and understanding are invaluable when dealing with struggling or challenging students. You provide support, encouragement, and guidance to help them reach their goals. Your caring and compassion are vital traits for effective teaching.

When students feel understood and supported by their teachers, they become more engaged and motivated in their learning. Your empathy allows you to connect with your students on a personal level, fostering trust and respect. Moreover, your empathetic nature helps you identify and address the emotional needs of your students, contributing to a positive learning environment.

Teaching can be challenging and frustrating at times, especially when working with academically or behaviorally struggling students. Your agreeableness shines through as you remain patient and tolerant. Your ability to avoid confrontation and competition allows you to focus on working together to achieve common goals. This fosters a supportive and collegial work environment, benefiting both teachers and students.

Overall, your agreeable nature and the accompanying traits make you an ideal candidate for the teaching profession. Your empathy, communication skills, patience, tolerance, and collaborative nature contribute to a positive and supportive learning environment. It is crucial to recognize and value these traits in the recruitment and training of teachers. By prioritizing the development of these traits, we can create a more inclusive and effective educational system.

Embrace your agreeable nature, dear teacher, and continue making a positive impact on the lives of your students. Your unique qualities contribute to a nurturing and empowering learning environment, shaping the future with compassion and collaboration.

Negative Traits

As an agreeable teacher, you possess numerous remarkable traits that benefit your teaching style. However, it's important to acknowledge that, like any other personality trait, there may be certain aspects that pose challenges. One negative aspect is the tendency to avoid conflict. While it may seem like a positive trait, it can lead to unresolved issues and problems in the classroom. Much like Abraham Wald with the planes in WW2, if you aren't willing to speak up and address issues that arise with students or colleagues, which can be difficult, it may result in a lack of progress or improvement that can benefit everyone. Avoiding confrontation can also lead to increased stress, and one of the drawbacks is struggling with setting boundaries. You prioritize maintaining harmony in your relationships, making it challenging for you to decline requests or demands from students, parents, or colleagues. This can lead to taking on too much responsibility, resulting in stress, burnout, and resentment towards others.

You may also be susceptible to manipulation and deception. Your trust and empathy towards others may make it challenging for you to recognize when someone is taking advantage of you or your resources, leading to feelings of frustration and resentment towards others.

Giving negative feedback to students can also be a struggle for highly agreeable teachers. You may avoid providing constructive criticism or feedback that could help students improve because you are concerned about hurting their feelings or damaging their self-esteem. This can result in students not reaching their full potential and can lead to frustration and burnout for you as a teacher.

Finally, it can be challenging for you to assert your own needs and opinions in the classroom. This can lead to a lack of autonomy and control over your own teaching practices, negatively impacting your job satisfaction and overall well-being. It is important to recognize the value of your opinions and ideas and communicate them respectfully and assertively with others.

Implications for Teachers

You bring many strengths and abilities to your role. Your approachability, empathy, and ability to build strong relationships with your students are highly effective. However, it's important to strike a balance by incorporating more assertiveness into your teaching approach. Throughout the book, we will emphasize the significance of developing assertiveness skills to help you unleash your full potential as an educator.

Assertiveness is a valuable skill for teachers, enabling you to clearly communicate your expectations and assert your authority while maintaining respect and empathy towards your students. It empowers you to set boundaries, enforce rules, and foster a positive and collaborative learning environment. By being assertive, you can confidently handle challenging situations, effectively manage disruptive behavior, and establish a sense of safety and structure in your classroom.

Embracing assertiveness has numerous benefits. It leads to improved student behavior, greater academic success, and higher overall job satisfaction for you as a teacher. Developing assertiveness skills empowers you to create a more fulfilling and successful career while helping your students reach their full potential and be their very best.

So, let us embark on this journey together, as we explore and cultivate your assertiveness skills. Through the strategies and insights in this book, you will unlock new levels of confidence and effectiveness in your teaching, creating a brighter future for both yourself and your students.

 Assertiveness Toolbox

1. Gratitude Journaling: Keep a gratitude journal where you write down at least one instance each day where your agreeableness made a positive impact in your teaching. This activity helps cultivate a mindset of appreciation for your agreeable qualities and their positive effects on others. Remember being highly agreeable has positive traits as well and impacting others' lives helps keep you inspired too!

2. Reflect on a recent interaction with a student, colleague, or parent. How did your positive traits, such as empathy or cooperation, influence your communication and assertiveness in that situation?

3. Take a moment to reflect on your overall job satisfaction and well-being as a teacher. How do your positive traits contribute to your happiness and effectiveness in the classroom? Are there areas where you can further develop your assertiveness to enhance your professional fulfillment?

2

From Passive to Powerful

Unleashing the Potential of Assertive Teaching

In *Freedom Writers*, Erin Gruwell, a newly hired teacher at a racially divided high school in Long Beach, California, is tasked with teaching a diverse group of students who are struggling academically and socially. Erin quickly realizes that her students have experienced profound trauma, including gang violence, racism, and poverty.

In one scene, Erin teaches her class about the Holocaust, hoping to inspire her students to see the impact of hatred and intolerance. However, the students initially display a lack of interest and respect for the topic, making racist comments and refusing to engage with the lesson.

Erin's assertiveness becomes evident when she refuses to ignore this behavior. Instead, she addresses the issue head-on, telling the students that their behavior is unacceptable and that she will not tolerate it in her classroom. Her assertiveness establishes a clear boundary, demonstrating that she will not allow disrespectful or intolerant behavior.

Erin takes the lesson further by bringing in Holocaust survivors to speak to the class. This powerful experience helps the students understand the severity of hatred and intolerance and the impact it can have on individuals and society as a whole.

Through her assertiveness, Erin creates a safe and respectful learning environment in which her students can learn and

DOI: 10.4324/9781003453796-2

grow. Her students are made aware of the boundaries and expectations she has set, and they understand that their actions have consequences. This encourages accountability and helps to establish a sense of responsibility in the classroom.

The scene is a powerful turning point for both Ms. Gruwell and her students. From that moment on, Ms. Gruwell is more assertive and sets clear boundaries with her students, while also continuing to connect with them on a personal level. The students begin to see her in a new light, and they start to make positive changes in their own lives. It's a powerful reminder of the importance of being assertive in the classroom and how it can also help us connect with our students and inspire them to be their best selves.

As teachers, we realize the importance of empathy, compassion, and even affirming our students. However, we also need to be able to create a safe and productive learning environment which depends on our capacity to communicate effectively, manage our classrooms, and establish clear boundaries with our students. This is where assertiveness comes in. Assertiveness is the ability to communicate our needs, opinions, and expectations in a clear and respectful manner, while also respecting the needs and rights of others.

Teaching is a profession that requires a combination of knowledge, skills, and personal qualities. Teachers are responsible for educating and guiding students towards success, but they also face several challenges that can impact their own job satisfaction and performance. These challenges include managing difficult students, communicating with parents, dealing with colleagues, and balancing a heavy workload.

Because many teachers are empathetic, affirmational, dislike conflict, have a hard time saying no, and are other-focused, they are often not as assertive as they could be. However, teachers need assertiveness skills in order to be their most effective. Assertive teachers are able to set clear boundaries, manage conflicts effectively, and build positive relationships with students, colleagues, and parents. They also demonstrate confidence in their decision-making and take responsibility for their actions. Overall, assertiveness is an important skill for teachers to have as it helps them to effectively lead and create a positive learning environment.

In this chapter, we will explore the benefits of teachers becoming more assertive. We will discuss how assertiveness can help teachers manage their classroom, communicate with parents, deal with colleagues, and balance their workload. We will also examine why some teachers struggle with assertiveness and examine strategies for teachers to develop their assertiveness skills.

What Does It Mean to Be Assertive?

Having been in the educational field for 30 years, I have found that there seems to be a major misconception about assertiveness. Assertiveness is often confused with aggression, rudeness, and hostility, however, assertiveness is distinct from these behaviors. It also does not involve domination, disrespect, or disregarding others' feelings and rights.

But assertiveness refers to the ability to express one's thoughts, feelings, opinions, needs, and boundaries in a direct and respectful manner.

> Assertiveness is the middle ground between being passive or aggressive and the perfect balance between being other-focused and self-focused.

It involves confidently communicating your ideas while considering the rights and feelings of others. Here are some key characteristics and behaviors associated with assertiveness:

- Clear communication: Assertive individuals express themselves clearly, using direct and concise language. They avoid vague or ambiguous statements, ensuring their message is understood by others.
- Respect for oneself and others: Assertiveness involves recognizing and respecting one's own needs and rights, as well as those of others. It's about finding a balance between advocating for oneself and considering the perspectives and boundaries of others.

- Confidence: Assertive individuals have confidence in their abilities and opinions. They believe in their own worth and express themselves without undermining or belittling others.
- Active listening: Being assertive also means being an active listener. Assertive individuals pay attention to others, show empathy, and demonstrate a genuine interest in understanding different viewpoints.
- Non-aggressive expression: Assertiveness is different from aggression. It does not involve hostility, intimidation, or disrespect. Assertive individuals express themselves assertively without resorting to aggressive or confrontational behavior.
- Boundary setting: Assertiveness includes the ability to set and maintain personal boundaries. This means communicating your limits, saying "no" when necessary, and respecting the boundaries of others.
- Conflict resolution: Assertive individuals are skilled at resolving conflicts in a constructive manner. They approach conflicts with a problem-solving mindset, seeking mutually beneficial solutions while considering the needs and feelings of all parties involved.

Assertiveness skills offer numerous benefits to you as a teacher. By developing assertiveness, you can effectively manage your classroom, communicate with your students, balance your authority with empathy, collaborate with colleagues and parents, manage stress, and promote your professional growth. Assertiveness helps you establish clear expectations and boundaries in the classroom, resulting in improved classroom management and a positive learning environment. You can confidently communicate instructions, feedback, and expectations to your students, enhancing their understanding and engagement.

Maintaining a balance between your authority as an educator and empathy for your students allows you to create a supportive and respectful classroom atmosphere. Furthermore, assertiveness facilitates effective collaboration with your colleagues and parents, leading to productive partnerships and better outcomes for your students. It also equips you with the skills to manage stress and maintain a healthy work-life balance by expressing your needs and setting boundaries. By advocating for yourself, seeking professional development opportunities, and confidently expressing your ideas and opinions, you can foster your own professional growth and advancement. Ultimately, embracing assertiveness empowers you to excel in your role, create positive learning environments, and nurture your own professional development.

The Importance of Teachers Developing Assertive Skills

As a teacher, you play a crucial role in the education and development of your students. However, you may feel like your voice is not heard and that you have no input in the decisions that affect your profession. It's important to recognize that you have the right to be heard and to assert your needs and concerns.

Assertiveness is a communication style where you express your thoughts, feelings, and needs in a clear, confident, and respectful manner, while also acknowledging the rights and needs of others. This style of communication can be crucial in establishing a positive classroom environment, managing behavior, and advocating for yourself and your students.

To be assertive, you need to have a clear understanding of your own beliefs, values, and needs and be able to communicate them effectively to others. You can achieve this by using "I" statements to express your own perspective, setting clear boundaries and expectations, and standing up for yourself and your students when necessary.

In the classroom, being assertive can help you set clear expectations and boundaries for your students. You can achieve this by establishing rules and consequences for behavior, communicating these expectations consistently and clearly to students, and enforcing these rules in a firm but fair manner.

Assertiveness can also be useful in managing disruptive behavior in the classroom. By communicating clearly and assertively with students who are exhibiting challenging behavior, you can prevent these behaviors from escalating and becoming more disruptive. This can create a more positive and productive learning environment for all students.

Last, being assertive can help you advocate for yourself and your students. By communicating assertively with parents, administrators, and other stakeholders, you can ensure that your needs and the needs of your students are being met. This can involve advocating for resources and support, communicating concerns or issues in a clear and respectful manner, and standing up for yourself and your students when necessary.

In conclusion, being assertive as a teacher can have many benefits, including establishing a positive classroom environment, managing behavior, and advocating for yourself and your students. By developing your assertiveness skills, you can become more confident and effective in your role as a teacher and help create a more positive and supportive learning experience for your students.

Reasons That May Hinder Teachers Becoming More Assertive

As a teacher, you may not have received adequate training or support on how to manage difficult classroom situations or assert yourself in front of students. This can lead to a lack of confidence and hesitation to take action when necessary. It is important to advocate for yourself and seek out professional development opportunities to develop your assertiveness skills.

Fear of Negative Consequences: You may worry that being too assertive could lead to conflict with students, parents, or administrators. This fear can be particularly acute if you are new or inexperienced and have not yet developed the skills and confidence needed to navigate difficult situations. It is important to remember that assertiveness is a valuable skill and that standing up for yourself and your students is important.

Personal Characteristics or Traits: Your personal characteristics or traits can also affect your ability to be assertive in the classroom. For example, if you are naturally introverted or shy, you may find it challenging to assert yourself in front of a class of students. Similarly, if you have a history of being bullied or intimidated, you may struggle with assertiveness due to past traumas. It is important to recognize and understand these factors and work to develop strategies to overcome them.

Cultural and Gender Stereotypes: Cultural and gender stereotypes can also play a role in your assertiveness. For example, as a woman teacher, you may be perceived as less assertive than your male counterparts due to societal expectations and gender stereotypes. Similarly, if you come from a cultural background that values politeness and deference, you may find it difficult to assert yourself in the classroom. It is important to challenge these stereotypes and work to develop your own assertiveness style that is authentic to you.

Lack of Autonomy: If you feel that you lack autonomy in your classroom, you may struggle with assertiveness. For example, if you are required to follow strict lesson plans or teaching methods, you may feel constrained in your ability to assert yourself and make decisions that are best for your students. Additionally, if you feel that your input is not valued or that your opinions are not taken into account, you may be less likely to assert yourself in the classroom. It is important to advocate for yourself and work to find ways to increase your autonomy.

Burnout: If you are overworked or overwhelmed, you may struggle with assertiveness as you may lack the energy or motivation to confront difficult situations. Burnout can lead to a lack of engagement, motivation, and assertiveness, which can have negative consequences on both you and your students. It is important to prioritize self-care and seek support when needed to prevent burnout.

Classroom Management Challenges: If you struggle with classroom management, you may also struggle with assertiveness. If you feel that you are not able to effectively manage your classroom, you may be hesitant to assert yourself for fear of losing control of the class or exacerbating the situation. It is important to work on developing effective classroom management strategies and seek support when needed.

Lack of Trust: If you feel that you do not have the support or trust of your colleagues or administrators, you may struggle with assertiveness. If you feel that your actions will not be supported or that you will be criticized for asserting yourself, you may be less likely to do so. It is important to build relationships and trust with your colleagues and administrators and to advocate for yourself and your students.

Focus on Relationship Building: While relationships are important, it is also important to be assertive when necessary to maintain a positive and effective learning environment. Prioritizing relationship building is important, but it should not come at the expense of assertiveness. It is important to find a balance between building positive relationships with your students and being assertive when necessary.

The Consequences of Lack of Assertiveness

As a teacher, it's essential to understand that a lack of assertiveness can have severe consequences for both you and your students. If you're too lenient or accommodating, students may take advantage of the situation, leading to a decline in discipline, performance, and achievement. This can lead to a lack of respect for your authority, and students may not take your lessons seriously, resulting in a lack of engagement and motivation.

Furthermore, a lack of assertiveness can take a toll on your well-being, leading to stress, burnout, and a feeling of being overwhelmed. You may find yourself working longer hours, dealing with more problems, and feeling dissatisfied with your job. This can result in difficulty confronting disruptive students or addressing problematic behavior that affects the entire class.

You may avoid conflict or be too lenient in your discipline, fearing that you may upset the student or damage the relationship.

When you lack assertiveness, you may also struggle to communicate your needs and expectations clearly to your students, colleagues, and parents. This can lead to resentment and feelings of undervaluation. However, instead of addressing these issues directly, you may engage in passive-aggressive behaviors such as procrastination, sarcasm, or intentionally failing to meet expectations. These behaviors can damage relationships and lead to burnout, decreased motivation, and poor job satisfaction.

To avoid the negative consequences of passive-aggressive behavior, it's important to develop your assertiveness skills. By learning to communicate your needs and expectations effectively, you can avoid becoming resentful and passive-aggressive. Instead, you can address issues constructively and directly, leading to stronger relationships, improved job satisfaction, and enhanced performance.

Strategies to Develop Your Assertiveness Skills

Developing assertiveness skills is crucial to create a positive and productive learning environment. Here is a list of strategies to help you develop your assertiveness skills:

- Engage in self-reflection to gain insight into your communication style and identify areas where you may feel less assertive. Recognize specific situations or interactions that require improvement and take targeted action to enhance your assertiveness.
- Set clear expectations by effectively communicating your expectations, rules, and boundaries to your students from the beginning. Ensure they understand what is expected of them and the consequences of not meeting those expectations. This promotes a structured and respectful classroom environment.
- Practice assertive communication techniques such as using "I" statements, expressing your needs and concerns

calmly and directly, and actively listening to students' perspectives. Developing these skills allows you to effectively communicate your ideas and address challenges assertively.

- Engage in role-playing activities and observe assertive behavior in colleagues or mentors. By practicing assertive responses and witnessing how others effectively communicate assertively, you can learn valuable techniques and gain confidence.
- Seek assertiveness training or attend workshops that focus on developing assertiveness skills. These professional development opportunities provide guidance, techniques, and practical exercises to strengthen your assertiveness in various situations.
- Build your self-confidence through personal development activities, positive self-talk, and recognizing your strengths as an educator. Increased self-confidence empowers you to be more assertive in your communication and actions.
- Develop active listening skills to understand students' perspectives and concerns. This allows you to respond assertively, address their needs effectively, and foster a supportive learning environment.
- Regularly seek feedback from students, colleagues, or mentors to gain valuable insights into how you come across in different situations. This feedback helps you identify areas for improvement and refine your assertiveness skills.
- Learn to manage your emotions effectively and respond assertively rather than reactively. Take a moment to pause, breathe, and think before responding to challenging situations. This promotes assertive communication and prevents escalation.
- Gradually expose yourself to assertive situations, starting with less challenging scenarios and progressively engaging in more difficult ones. This approach allows you to build your assertiveness skills over time, gaining confidence and proficiency.

- By implementing these strategies and actively developing your assertiveness skills, you can create a positive, engaging, and effective learning environment for both yourself and your students.

 Assertiveness Toolbox:

1. Reflect on the benefits of assertiveness: Reflect on your work and identify specific situations where assertiveness would be helpful, such as communicating with parents or addressing student misbehavior.

2. Practice saying "no": High agreeableness teachers often have a hard time saying "no" to requests, which can lead to overcommitment and burnout. They can practice saying "no" to small requests to build their confidence and comfort level.

3. Use assertive language: High agreeableness teachers can use assertive language to express their needs and opinions, such as "I think" or "I feel." They can also use "I" statements to communicate their perspective without blaming or accusing others.

3

Finding the Strength Within

Empowering Teachers Through Self-awareness
and Confidence

In the movie *Rocky*, there is a powerful scene where Rocky Balboa, played by Sylvester Stallone, is training in the gym and begins to reflect on his own abilities and limitations. He is preparing for the fight of his life against the heavyweight champion of the world, Apollo Creed, and he is feeling overwhelmed and unsure of himself.

As Rocky is punching the heavy bag, he starts to think about his opponent and all the things that make him a great fighter. He thinks about Apollo's speed, power, and precision and begins to doubt whether he can compete with him.

But then something shifts in Rocky's mindset. He realizes that he has been focusing too much on Apollo's strengths and not enough on his own. He starts to hit the bag with more force and determination and begins to reflect on his own abilities as a fighter.

He remembers his own strength, resilience, and determination and begins to tap into his own inner power. He starts to train with a new intensity, focusing on what he can do rather than what his opponent can do.

This moment of self-awareness is a turning point for Rocky. He realizes that he has been underestimating himself and that he has the ability to compete with the best. He taps into his own

DOI: 10.4324/9781003453796-3

strength and potential and approaches the fight with a newfound confidence and determination.

In the end, Rocky goes the distance in the ring with Apollo, proving to himself and the world that he is a true contender. This scene is a powerful example of the importance of self-awareness in recognizing one's own strengths and using them to achieve success, even in the face of seemingly insurmountable challenges.

I think teachers often feel like Rocky because we feel like we face insurmountable challenges in education: high expectations, with limited resources, support, and encouragement to reach our potential. However, to reach our full potential, we must be confident in ourselves and the strengths we bring to the table to be our best.

Remember that, for the most part, teachers are other-focused. We are constantly affirming, encouraging, and helping others become their best. So we either don't take time to focus on self, or we never even realize the importance of focusing on self. Therefore, this chapter will help you change the lens through which you view yourself. We will focus on building strengths, becoming more self-aware, and building self-confidence so that you will be a more assertive and effective teacher. It is not selfish to focus on self, but rather it is the key to maximizing your potential and bringing your best to every facet of your role.

Building Self-confidence

You possess a unique set of talents, knowledge, and experiences that make you a remarkable teacher. Recognizing and embracing your strengths is a powerful pathway towards building self-confidence in the classroom. By tapping into these areas of expertise and acknowledging your accomplishments, you can cultivate a strong sense of self-assurance that will positively impact your teaching practice and student engagement.

They say there are two important days in your life: the day you were born and the day you realize why you were born. We were all born with purpose. Our purpose is typically found when we identify and develop our talents and our passions. In fact, there is not much more inspiring than identifying and living out your purpose.

The problem is that, in our culture, we are always focused on our weaknesses. Commercials are geared towards what we are missing or what we need to be better. Even in education, we often see so much emphasis placed on correcting weaknesses rather than on developing strengths. And the harder something is to do, then the more valued we think it must be, because it took hard work and rigor to make it better! And so, we rarely value our strengths and talents because they do come easier for us, which is ironic because our strengths are what set us apart, what make us stand out.

Understanding Your Strengths

Strengths and talents are qualities and abilities that come naturally to an individual, which they can use to excel in certain areas or tasks. A strength can be a specific skill or knowledge, while a talent can be an innate ability or inclination towards a particular activity or subject.

In essence, strengths and talents are those things that we are particularly good at, enjoy doing, and can leverage to achieve success in our personal or professional lives. They can include a wide range of attributes such as creativity, critical thinking, communication skills, leadership abilities, and technical expertise, among others. What is interesting is that while we all have talents and strengths, they are rarely a focus of our personal development.

For several years, I taught graduate level leadership courses in a MEd program for leadership certification. I taught a course that focused on helping educators identify and develop their leadership strengths. My students were veteran teachers with anywhere from 3 or 4 years of experience to some with 20 years of experience. One of the first activities I had them do was take a Strengths Finder assessment, which helps identities your top five leadership strengths. I would then have them write a reflection paper on the results of the assessment.

But do you know what surprised me or maybe I should say saddened me the most about the process? It was the number of adults educators who told me they had never really thought about having leadership talents or strengths. In fact, most said they had never really thought about what strengths they had at all. Imagine professionals who really have never thought about their leadership strengths. One of the main reasons that we do not focus on our strengths is because we are a highly deficit-based culture. By that I mean we focus too much on weaknesses or areas of growth. Think about it; we often value or place value on things that are hard to do. We say that if something is of value it must be hard, it must require vigor or grit. However actually the opposite of this is true. Because it is actually our strengths that give us our value, and because they are our strengths, they actually come easy to us. But because they come easy to us, we often don't realize their value. We teach classes with this deficit mindset. For example, most teacher evaluations focus on areas of growth or weaknesses; they rarely focus on our strengths and developing them to become our very best. We do the same thing with students. For example, if a student does poorly in math but does well in reading, we focus on helping them become a little better in math, instead of helping them become excellent in reading.

This is an area that I greatly emphasize during my PD sessions, because I ask teachers if they can quickly identify four or five of their talents or strengths, and most of them struggle many times to just come up with one or two. Ironically if I ask them to identify three or four strengths or talents of their teammates, they can name them off rapidly. Isn't it interesting that we can see the talents and strengths and others but often can't see them in ourselves? I believe this is because of the cultural emphasis on weaknesses, which can have a significant impact on how individuals perceive themselves. When people are constantly told to focus on their weaknesses, they may begin to feel inadequate and believe that they have little to offer. This negative self-image can make it difficult for individuals to recognize and appreciate their own strengths.

Furthermore, individuals may not even be aware of their own strengths due to this cultural emphasis on weaknesses. When people are constantly told to improve their weaknesses, they may not spend enough time reflecting on their strengths. As a result, they may not be able to recognize their own unique talents and abilities.

Maximizing Potential Through Strengths

Improving our strengths can have a significant impact on our success in all areas of our lives. One way that focusing on our strengths can make us more successful is by building our confidence. When we know what we are good at and are able to utilize our strengths, we feel more confident in our abilities. This confidence can lead us to take on new challenges, pursue our goals more vigorously, and ultimately achieve greater success. By building our confidence through our strengths, we are able to overcome obstacles and achieve more than we might have otherwise thought possible.

In addition to building our confidence, improving our strengths can also make us more productive. When we leverage our strengths in our work, we are able to complete tasks more quickly and effectively. This can lead to increased efficiency, greater output, and, ultimately, greater success. By focusing on our strengths, we can also find ways to delegate tasks that play to the strengths of others, allowing us to work more collaboratively and achieve more together.

Improving our strengths can make us more successful by improving our relationships. When we understand and communicate our strengths effectively, we are better able to collaborate with others who have complementary strengths. This can lead to more productive partnerships and teams, and, ultimately, greater success. Additionally, by focusing on our strengths, we can better understand the strengths of others, leading to more meaningful connections and relationships. Ultimately, by improving our strengths, we are able to achieve greater success in all areas of our lives, from our personal relationships to our careers.

In order to reach your full potential, you must be able to identify and leverage your strengths. In fact, there was a Gallup poll that showed that when employees, which included teachers, felt like their talents and strengths were utilized and that they were valued in their role, they were six times more engaged in their jobs. You read that right, six times more engaged in their job and they were also three times more likely to say that they had a higher quality of life. And as we all know if your work life is going well it often carries over into our home life. When people recognize their strengths, they can focus their time and energy on activities that allow them to thrive. This can lead to increased satisfaction and fulfillment in both personal and professional pursuits.

Identifying Your Strengths

As a teacher, the first step in identifying your strengths is self-reflection. Reflect on your experiences, skills, and interests to identify your strengths. Ask yourself questions such as:

- What activities do you enjoy doing the most?
- What feedback have you received from students or colleagues about what you do well?
- What are your proudest accomplishments as a teacher?

You can also seek feedback from colleagues, mentors, or supervisors to gain insights into your strengths. Feedback can help you identify areas where you excel and areas where you may need to improve. You can also use self-assessment tools or personality tests to identify your strengths and weaknesses.

Once you have identified your strengths, you can work to develop them further. Here are some strategies that you can use to develop your strengths:

1. Professional development: Participate in professional development opportunities that are aligned with your strengths. For example, if you excel in using technology in the classroom, attend a technology-focused workshop to develop your skills further.
2. Coaching or mentoring: Work with a coach or mentor to identify and develop your strengths. A coach or mentor can provide guidance, support, and feedback to help you enhance your strengths.

3. Collaboration: Collaborate with colleagues who have complementary strengths. Collaborating with others can help you learn new skills and approaches and can enhance your own strengths.

4. Practice: Practice your strengths in the classroom by incorporating them into your lesson plans and teaching practice. For example, if you are skilled at project-based learning, incorporate more project-based activities into your curriculum.

5. Reflection: Reflect on your practice and evaluate the effectiveness of your strengths. This can help you identify areas for improvement and refine your teaching practice.

Developing your strengths can benefit both you and your students. For you, developing your strengths can enhance your job satisfaction and lead to a more fulfilling career. You may feel more confident, engaged, and motivated. For your students, you are better able to provide high-quality instruction and support. By leveraging your strengths, you can create a positive and engaging learning environment that supports student growth and success.

Identifying and developing strengths is a critical component of professional development for teachers. By taking the time to reflect on your practice, seek feedback, and participate in professional development opportunities, you can identify your strengths and develop them further. Developing strengths can lead to a more fulfilling career for you and better outcomes for your students.

"When you leverage your strengths in the classroom," says Carol Vernon, certified executive coach, "you are more naturally engaged with your students and students know it!" "One way to identify them to yourself," says Vernon in an interview with We Are Teachers, "is to identify the activities that you do regularly that make you most energized and engaged." (2013) Strengths are the traits that you find yourself coming back to again and again, regardless of what you may have originally planned. Focusing on your strengths not only helps you be inspired but to be inspiring to your students!

Becoming More Self-aware

As a teacher, it is crucial to develop self-awareness to reflect on your own thoughts, feelings, and actions and how they impact your teaching practice and interactions with students. By having a high level of self-awareness, you can understand your own biases, strengths, and weaknesses and how these can affect your effectiveness as a teacher. This can lead to improved teaching practices, increased student engagement, and a more positive learning environment.

By becoming more self-aware, you can experience several benefits that can positively impact your teaching practice. First, it can help you identify tendencies towards people-pleasing and conflict avoidance, which are common traits among individuals high in agreeableness. Recognizing these tendencies can help you to develop assertiveness and boundary-setting skills, which can help you navigate difficult situations with students, colleagues, and parents more effectively. This can lead to greater respect from others, as well as improved communication and collaboration within the school community.

Self-awareness can help you strike a balance between the desire to please others and your own needs and goals as an educator. By reflecting on your own values and priorities, you can ensure that your teaching practices align with your personal goals and the needs of your students, rather than simply conforming to the expectations of others. This can lead to greater job satisfaction and a sense of purpose in your work. Additionally, self-awareness can help you better manage stress and avoid burnout by recognizing when you are taking on too much and learning to say no to excessive demands on your time and energy.

Benefits of Becoming Self-aware

As a teacher, self-awareness is a crucial skill that can help you better understand yourself and your behavior. One way self-awareness can benefit you is by helping you identify your emotional triggers and how you respond to them. For instance, if you get frustrated when students do not follow instructions, self-awareness can help you learn to respond assertively by setting clear boundaries and communicating expectations more effect-ively.

Another benefit of self-awareness is that it allows you to identify your strengths and weaknesses. Understanding your strengths and weaknesses can aid you in making assertive decisions that align with your values and beliefs. By leveraging your strengths, you can assert your position on issues that matter to you and achieve your goals.

Self-awareness can also help you recognize the impact of your behavior on others. By reflecting on your interactions with others, you can identify areas where you need to be more assert-ive in order to advocate for your students and yourself. For example, you may realize that your behavior is impacting your students negatively and take steps to change your behavior to create a more positive learning environment.

Finally, self-awareness can help you respond assertively to challenging situations. By recognizing your emotions and choosing appropriate responses, you can learn to respond assert-ively to conflicts with colleagues or parents. For example, if you tend to avoid conflict, self-awareness can help you learn to assert your position respectfully and confidently in a difficult conver-sation.

Practical Strategies for Developing Self-awareness as an Assertive Teacher

As a teacher, there are various aspects of personal growth and well-being that can significantly impact your effectiveness in the classroom. In addition to developing teaching skills and subject knowledge, paying attention to your own self-awareness and communication abilities is crucial. This section explores six key strategies that can enhance your self-awareness and improve your communication as a teacher. From practicing mindfulness and seeking feedback to developing emotional intelligence and setting boundaries, each technique offers valuable insights and practical steps to support your professional and personal growth.

1. Mindfulness: Practice mindfulness to increase your self-awareness. Engage in techniques like meditation and

deep breathing to cultivate the ability to notice your thoughts, emotions, and physical sensations. This heightened awareness will help you understand how these internal experiences influence your behavior and communication.

2. Feedback: Seek feedback from colleagues, mentors, or even students to gain valuable insights into your behavior and communication style. Ask for specific feedback on interactions or request general feedback on your teaching practice. Approach feedback with an open mind, using it constructively to enhance your skills and effectiveness.

3. Emotional Intelligence: Develop emotional intelligence by learning to recognize and manage your own emotions as well as the emotions of others. Understanding others' emotions enables you to respond compassionately and constructively, fostering positive connections and effective communication.

4. Prioritize Self: Make self-care a priority to regulate your emotions and respond constructively to challenging situations. Dedicate time to physical exercise, meditation, or spending time in nature, which will enhance your self-awareness and enable you to be an assertive teacher.

5. Set Boundaries: Establish clear boundaries that communicate what is acceptable and what is not. Clearly communicate your expectations and limits to others, and be willing to enforce consequences when those boundaries are crossed. Setting limits on communication after work hours is one example of maintaining a healthy work-life balance.

6. Beware of Negative Self-Comparison: Beware of negative self-comparison, as it can have significant implications for your professional and personal well-being as a teacher. Constantly measuring yourself against others and perceiving yourself as falling short can lead to feelings of inadequacy and low self-esteem. These negative emotions can negatively impact your confidence in the classroom and hinder your ability to effectively engage and inspire your students. Excessive self-comparison

can distract you from focusing on your own growth and development. Instead of setting meaningful goals based on your individual strengths and areas for improvement, you may become preoccupied with trying to emulate someone else's success, thereby overlooking your own unique talents and contributions.

In the pursuit of becoming a more effective and fulfilled teacher, it is important to prioritize self-awareness and effective communication. By incorporating mindfulness practices into your daily routine, developing emotional intelligence, prioritizing self-care, setting clear boundaries, and avoiding negative self-comparison, you can cultivate a deeper understanding of yourself and improve your interactions with others. These strategies not only contribute to your professional growth but also enhance your overall well-being, creating a positive and empowering teaching environment. Remember, by continuously investing in your own personal development, you can become an even more impactful and successful teacher.

Understand Your Wants and Needs

Unfortunately, many teachers are so other-focused that they often don't know even know what they really want or need, which may be the most important aspect of self-awareness. You naturally prioritize the needs and wants of others. Your focus is on maintaining harmony, fostering positive relationships, and avoiding conflict. This tendency may lead you to invest more energy in understanding and meeting the needs of others rather than identifying your own wants and needs.

You may feel discomfort when it comes to conflict. Expressing your own desires may seem disruptive or confrontational, which makes it challenging for you to recognize and assert your own needs.

There might be a fear of being perceived as selfish. You have a strong desire to be seen as considerate and helpful, and you worry that prioritizing your own wants and needs could be viewed as selfish or inconsiderate. This fear can create internal resistance, making it difficult for you to acknowledge and pursue your own desires.

Over time, you may have developed a habitual pattern of self-neglect. Putting others first has become second nature, and you may not even be aware of your own desires. This lack of self-awareness can contribute to neglecting your own wants and needs.

You may rely heavily on external validation and approval to feel a sense of self-worth. Consequently, you prioritize meeting the expectations and needs of others, seeking validation from external sources rather than focusing on your own wants and needs.

Recognizing these challenges is an important step towards reclaiming your own wants and needs. By developing self-awareness, setting boundaries, and practicing assertiveness, you can strike a balance between caring for others and taking care of yourself. Remember that prioritizing your own well-being is not selfish but essential for your overall happiness and effectiveness as a teacher.

Identifying your wants: Begin by reflecting on your teaching experiences and the aspects that bring you joy and fulfillment. Consider the following questions:

- What teaching methods or strategies do you genuinely enjoy using?
- Are there specific topics or subjects that ignite your passion as an educator?
- Do you have any aspirations for your teaching career or professional development?
- What aspects of teaching make you feel most fulfilled and satisfied?

Based on your reflections, shift your focus to your wants as a teacher. Ask yourself:

- What are your aspirations for your teaching practice and professional growth?

- Are there any particular teaching methods, technologies, or resources you would like to incorporate?
- What goals or achievements would bring you a sense of personal and professional fulfillment?

Identifying Your Needs

Begin by reflecting on your teaching experiences and the areas where you need support or fulfillment. Consider the following questions:

- Are there any resources or materials that would enhance your teaching effectiveness?
- What kind of support or guidance do you need from colleagues, mentors, or administrators?
- Do you require specific professional development opportunities to meet your needs?
- Are there any aspects of your work environment that you find challenging or unsupportive?

Examine your well-being: Shift your focus to your personal well-being as a teacher. Ask yourself:

- What are your basic physical and emotional needs that should be met in your teaching environment?
- Do you require time for self-care, relaxation, or pursuing personal interests?
- Are there any boundaries you need to establish to maintain a healthy work-life balance?
- What support do you need to prevent burnout and maintain your overall well-being?

Engaging in these self-reflection activities can help you identify your wants and needs, enabling you to make informed decisions, advocate for yourself, and seek the necessary support and resources to thrive in your teaching career. By taking the time to reflect on your experiences, aspirations, and areas where you need support, you gain clarity and a deeper understanding of what you truly desire as an educator. This self-awareness empowers you to make choices that align with your goals and values, communicate your needs assertively, and seek out opportunities for growth and fulfillment. Remember, prioritizing your wants and needs is essential for your overall well-being and effectiveness as a teacher.

Overcoming Imposter Syndrome

If you're a teacher, it's important to be aware of imposter syndrome, a phenomenon identified by psychologists Pauline Clance and Suzanne Imes in the 1970s. This belief that you are not as competent or qualified as others perceive you to be can lead to feelings of self-doubt, fear of failure, and a sense of fraudulence. As a teacher, you may feel under immense pressure to perform well, which can exacerbate these feelings.

As a result of imposter syndrome, you tend to be excessively self-critical and are your own worst critic. You may constantly doubt your abilities and skills, believing that you are not doing enough or that you are not good enough. This can lead to a fear of being exposed as a fraud, and you may feel like you need to work harder and prove yourself constantly.

Additionally, as a teacher with imposter syndrome, you may compare yourself to other teachers and feel like you are not measuring up. You may feel like your colleagues are more knowledgeable or successful, leading to feelings of inadequacy and self-doubt.

The constant self-criticism and fear of being exposed as a fraud can lead to negative emotions, such as anxiety and stress, which can affect your job performance and overall well-being.

If you are a teacher struggling with imposter syndrome, it can be challenging to overcome. However, there are several strategies you can use to regain your confidence and overcome these feelings of self-doubt. One effective method is to challenge your negative self-talk. When you hear yourself thinking negative thoughts, stop and ask yourself if they are based in reality or if they are just your inner critic speaking. Then, challenge those thoughts by reminding yourself of your accomplishments and positive feedback from others. This can help you reframe your thoughts and build a more positive self-image.

As we mentioned earlier, another helpful strategy is to focus on your strengths and skills. Instead of dwelling on your perceived shortcomings, make a list of the things you excel at and enjoy doing in your role as a teacher. This will help you shift your focus from self-doubt to self-affirmation. Additionally, seek feedback from your colleagues and students, and take note of positive comments or compliments they give you. This can help you see yourself through others' eyes and realize that you are doing a good job.

To overcome imposter syndrome, it's crucial for you to recognize and celebrate your own achievements and strengths, rather than fixating on perceived shortcomings. Seek support from colleagues, administrators, and mentors who can provide guidance and help build your confidence. Remember that you deserve to be in your position and that you bring unique skills and talents to your role as a teacher.

Taking care of yourself is essential to combat imposter syndrome. Prioritize self-care activities that promote your physical and emotional well-being, such as exercise, meditation, spending time with loved ones, and engaging in hobbies or activities that bring you joy and relaxation. By investing in self-care, you'll be better equipped to handle the demands of teaching and will be able to be more present for your students.

Practicing self-compassion is another powerful tool. Treat yourself with kindness, understanding, and forgiveness. Rather than dwelling on mistakes or flaws, recognize that they are a natural part of the learning process and an opportunity for growth. Embrace a mindset of self-acceptance and remember that everyone faces challenges and setbacks.

Challenge negative self-talk by questioning its validity and replacing it with positive and realistic thoughts. Reframe negative thoughts by focusing on your past successes, skills, and positive feedback from students and colleagues. Remind yourself that everyone has moments of self-doubt, and that doesn't diminish your capabilities as a teacher.

Remember, overcoming imposter syndrome is an ongoing process. Be patient with yourself, celebrate your achievements, and embrace your role as a capable and deserving teacher. With time and practice, you'll develop a stronger sense of self-confidence and authenticity in your profession.

Why You Should Celebrate Your Successes

Recognizing and celebrating your successes as a teacher can have a profound impact on your overall well-being, motivation, and classroom culture. By acknowledging your accomplishments and valuing your efforts, you not only boost your self-esteem but also inspire and motivate yourself to reach new heights. This guide explores the importance of celebrating your successes in the teaching profession, highlighting their benefits in terms of self-worth, motivation, classroom culture, reflection, and the acknowledgment of effort. It is important for you to celebrate your successes for several reasons:

Recognition and self-worth: By celebrating your successes, you can recognize your accomplishments and acknowledge your own abilities and hard work. This boosts your self-esteem and reinforces a positive self-image. By celebrating your successes, you affirm your value and worth as an educator, contributing to a healthy sense of self.

Motivation and inspiration: Celebrating your successes provides motivation and inspiration to continue striving for excellence. Recognizing your achievements can fuel your drive to set and achieve new goals. By celebrating your successes, you maintain a sense of enthusiasm, passion, and dedication to your profession. This motivation can positively impact your teaching approach and ultimately benefit your students.

Positive classroom culture: Celebrating your successes creates a positive classroom culture and fosters a supportive learning environment. By sharing and celebrating your own achievements, you model the importance of acknowledging and valuing accomplishments. This encourages students to do the same and promotes a growth mindset, where effort and progress are recognized and celebrated. A positive classroom culture enhances student engagement, confidence, and overall academic performance.

Reflection and growth: Celebrating your successes provides an opportunity for reflection and growth. By acknowledging your achievements, you can reflect on the strategies, efforts, and lessons learned that contributed to your success. This reflection allows you to identify areas of strength and areas for further development. Celebrating your successes becomes a platform for continuous improvement and personal growth as an educator.

Celebration of effort: celebrating your successes is not just about the result but also about acknowledging the effort and progress you made along the way. You may tend to focus on others' achievements, but celebrating your own successes is a way to recognize and honor your own hard work, dedication, and resilience. It validates your commitment to continuous improvement and serves as a reminder of your capabilities and impact as an educator.

In conclusion, celebrating your successes is important for you to recognize your achievements, maintain motivation, foster a positive classroom culture, promote growth, and honor your own efforts. By celebrating your successes, you reinforce your self-worth, inspire others, and contribute to a fulfilling and rewarding teaching experience.

Assertive Toolbox:

1. Self-assessment: use a self-assessment tool such as StrengthsFinders or personality test to identify your strengths. This can help you understand your unique strengths and talents that you bring to the table. You can then focus on developing them even more to be exponentially more successful.

2. Use positive self-talk: practice positive self-talk to reinforce your confidence and self-worth. Use affirmations and positive statements such as "I am a capable and confident teacher" or "I have the skills and knowledge to succeed

in the classroom." By cultivating a positive mindset, you can approach conflict with greater self-assurance.

3. Challenge imposter syndrome: recognize and address imposter syndrome by challenging negative self-talk, focusing on your strengths and accomplishments, seeking feedback and support, and practicing self-compassion.

4

Navigating Conflict with Confidence

Building Relationships and Resolving Issues with Assertiveness

If there was one person in history who had many challenges in becoming more assertive, it was Katherine Johnson. Her story is a remarkable one of assertiveness, determination, and brilliance in the face of adversity. Born in 1918 in White Sulphur Springs, West Virginia, she was one of the first African-American women to work as a mathematician at NASA.

Despite facing discrimination and segregation as a woman of color in the 1950s and 60s, Johnson was determined to make a difference in the field of space exploration. She was a skilled mathematician, and her calculations were critical to the success of many missions, including the Friendship 7 mission that made John Glenn the first American to orbit the Earth.

During this mission, there was a problem with the spacecraft's trajectory. Glenn himself had doubts about the computer's calculations, and he asked mission control to "get the girl" to recalculate the trajectory by hand. Katherine Johnson was that girl.

Despite facing immense pressure and a tight deadline, Katherine Johnson remained calm and focused as she recalculated the spacecraft's trajectory by hand. She factored in several variables that the computer had not considered, including the gravitational pull of the moon and other celestial bodies. Her calculations were critical to the success of the mission, and John Glenn safely returned to Earth.

Katherine Johnson's assertiveness was evident throughout her career. While Katherine was not necessarily a confrontational person, she was not afraid of conflict when it came to defending her ideas or advocating for herself. For example, despite facing discrimination and being told that she could not attend meetings or work on certain projects because of her race and gender, she persisted and fought for her right to be included. She broke barriers and paved the way for future generations of women and people of color in STEM fields, leaving a legacy that continues to inspire and motivate people around the world.

Growth Mindset

We all face obstacles, challenges, and barriers, which may keep us from becoming our best. When you embrace these barriers, a growth mindset encourages you to view them as opportunities for growth and improvement. As a teacher striving to be more assertive, you may encounter challenges such as overcoming self-doubt, managing conflicts, or asserting yourself in difficult situations. However, with a growth mindset, you will approach these challenges as valuable learning experiences, rather than becoming discouraged by them.

Embracing challenges is a key aspect of cultivating a growth mindset. Step out of your comfort zone and be willing to face the discomfort that comes with developing assertiveness. See challenges as opportunities for personal and professional growth, as they provide valuable learning experiences that can enhance your skills.

Persistence and effort are crucial in the journey towards assertiveness. Understand that growth requires consistent dedication and a willingness to invest time and energy in overcoming barriers. Recognize that improvement takes time, and with perseverance and continued practice, your assertiveness will develop.

Challenge fixed mindset beliefs that may hinder your assertiveness. Replace thoughts like "I should always avoid conflict" with growth mindset statements such as "I can learn to assert myself respectfully and maintain positive relationships." By challenging these beliefs, you open yourself up to new possibilities and empower yourself to take assertive actions.

Embrace discomfort as a catalyst for growth. Recognize that stepping outside of your comfort zone is necessary for personal and professional development. Embrace the discomfort that comes with assertiveness as an opportunity for growth and learning. View it as a skill that can be developed over time with practice and dedication.

Set incremental goals to track your progress in assertiveness. Break down the skill into smaller, achievable goals. Start with low-stakes situations and gradually work towards more challenging ones. Celebrate each step of progress, reinforcing the belief that assertiveness is a skill that can be developed through incremental achievements. For example,

1. Start with a low-stakes situation: begin by selecting a low-stakes situation where you can practice assertiveness. It could be as simple as expressing your opinion during a team meeting or assertively communicating your needs to a colleague. Choose a situation that feels manageable and less intimidating to build your confidence.

2. Define specific goals: break down the assertiveness skill into specific goals for the chosen situation. For example, you might aim to clearly state your perspective without hesitation, maintain a calm and confident tone throughout the conversation, and actively listen to others' viewpoints while expressing your own. By setting clear goals, you provide yourself with a roadmap for success.

3. Practice and reflect: engage in deliberate practice by role-playing the situation with a trusted colleague or in front of a mirror. Pay attention to your body language, tone of voice, and clarity of your message. Afterward, take time

to reflect on the experience. Identify areas where you excelled and areas that need improvement. Honest self-reflection will help you refine your approach.

4. Gradually increase the challenge: once you feel comfortable and confident in low-stakes situations, it's time to gradually raise the level of challenge. Select more demanding scenarios where you can assert yourself effectively. For instance, you could practice assertiveness during a difficult parent-teacher conference or address a classroom issue assertively with your students. Pushing yourself out of your comfort zone will facilitate further growth.

5. Set new goals: As you gain proficiency in assertiveness, set new, more advanced goals for higher-stakes situations. These goals might involve managing potential conflicts more effectively, calmly responding to resistance, or maintaining assertiveness while considering the needs and perspectives of others. Push yourself to achieve new levels of assertiveness.

Value the process of learning and engage in self-reflection. Reflect on your barriers to assertiveness and actively seek resources, strategies, and support to overcome them. Embrace a mindset of continuous learning, be open to new assertiveness techniques, and adjust your approach based on your experiences. Understand that growth requires ongoing learning and self-reflection.

Embrace mistakes and setbacks as opportunities for growth. Rather than viewing them as failures, see them as valuable learning experiences. Reflect on what went wrong, learn from your mistakes, and adjust your strategies accordingly. Use setbacks as steppingstones to further develop your assertiveness skills and build resilience.

By actively adopting a growth mindset and applying these strategies, you demonstrate a belief in your ability to change and improve. Embrace challenges, persist in your efforts, seek opportunities for learning, and view setbacks as part of the growth process. Through these actions, you will develop your assertiveness skills and create a positive and empowering environment for yourself and those around you.

Handling Conflict/Confrontation

Much like the word assertive is often seen in a negative light, confrontation is often viewed as a four-letter word as well, especially if you are empathetic, compassionate, and cooperative, valuing harmonious relationships above all else. This means you tend to prioritize maintaining harmony and avoid confrontation whenever possible.

However, there are instances where confrontation becomes unavoidable, even for someone with a highly agreeable disposition. It's important to recognize that constructive confrontation can lead to growth and resolution. By engaging in thoughtful and respectful conversations, you can address issues that arise within your classroom or professional relationships.

When confronted with situations that require addressing conflicts or differing opinions, it may be challenging for you to assert yourself. However, remember that confrontation doesn't have to be aggressive or confrontational in nature. You can approach these situations with empathy and compassion, seeking to understand different perspectives and finding common ground.

It's essential to recognize that healthy confrontation can lead to personal and professional growth. By addressing concerns or conflicts directly, you can maintain a positive and productive learning environment for your students. Open communication and constructive feedback can lead to better collaboration among colleagues and improved outcomes for everyone involved.

The reality is that even in the best school cultures, conflicts will arise. And whether we hate it or not, it is unavoidable, but it is how we deal with it that matters. While confronting someone is not really pleasant, it's something you must do as a teacher, and how you do it makes all the difference.

One trait of an assertive individual is that they are good at handling conflict and confrontation. This doesn't mean that they enjoy it or seek it out but that they have developed the skills to handle it in a positive light. Conflict is often seen as negative. But conflict is really a natural part of relationships and the key is not to avoid them but to handle them properly. When we understand how to influence conflict and confrontation, then there is very little we can't handle. These tough conversations can nurture deep professional learning as individuals and teams, explore new ideas for practice, as well as strengthen relationships among the team. However, they may also lead to conflict, especially when you have individuals with different strengths, perspectives, and experiences. Conflict, however, is not necessarily bad, as discussed in the communication chapter. In fact, team conflict can sometimes create better solutions. Of course, we don't want people who must argue with every idea just for the sake of argument, but if something doesn't seem as logical as it sounds, maybe there does need to be more discussion. Team conflict can lead to better practices or improved results. This concept is worth repeating because conflict is often seen as negative and divisive to teams. But the reality is you have people on your teams with different strengths, perspectives, and expertise, so some may identify issues that others don't see or there may simply be disagreements. I think of conflict as being kind of like stress. It's not that we will never encounter it, but it is how we deal with it that matters. While confronting someone is not particularly pleasant, it's something you must do as a leader, and how you do it makes all the difference. I think it is one of the reasons that I have been so successful in my career is that I learned early on how to deal with confrontation. In fact, this is one of my favorite topics to speak on because understanding how to deal with confrontation will make every leader's life so much easier, not just professionally but personally as well.

According to Dianna Booher, a communication expert and author of *Speak with Confidence*, you must believe that confrontation can be a positive situation. After all, confrontation handled well has many benefits which include:

- innovative solutions to problems
- improvements to the status quo
- stronger confidence in implementing ideas
- stronger relationships
- greater harmony
- improved communication

- better teamwork
- greater understanding
- increased engagement on the job
- strong passion and commitment to see success of the ideas developed (2017)

So don't shy away from conflict when it arises, but rather use the opportunity to build stronger relationships with your teachers. The reason confrontation is hard is that it is outside of our comfort zone. We let things build until emotions are high, and then we tend to overreact. Here are some great strategies to help you deal with conflict in a more assertive manner and make it a beneficial part of the communication process:

Focus on Being Proactive, Not Reactive

In the realm of education, conflicts are bound to arise among teachers, whether related to classroom management, instructional strategies, or interpersonal dynamics. When you face conflict, it is crucial for you to adopt a proactive approach rather than a reactive one. Here's why focusing on being proactive is essential in conflict resolution:

- Maintain a positive work environment: When you react impulsively to conflicts, it can escalate the situation and create a negative atmosphere among your colleagues. By being proactive, you can address issues early on and prevent them from festering into larger problems. This promotes a positive work environment where everyone feels respected and valued.
- Foster open communication: Proactively addressing conflicts encourages open and honest communication. Instead of allowing frustrations to build up, express your concerns respectfully and listen to others with an open mind. This approach creates opportunities for understanding, empathy, and finding common ground.
- Seek solutions and growth: Being proactive means actively seeking solutions rather than dwelling on the problem itself. Work collaboratively with your colleagues

to identify the underlying causes of conflicts and explore strategies to resolve them. This approach not only resolves immediate issues but also promotes your personal and professional growth.

By taking a proactive stance in conflict resolution, you can create a more harmonious and productive work environment where issues are addressed promptly and collaboratively. Remember, being proactive allows you to maintain a positive atmosphere, foster open communication, and seek growth and solutions for the benefit of yourself and your colleagues.

Focus on Relating, Not on Being Right

Conflicts can often become heated and emotional when individuals focus solely on proving themselves right. Instead, you should prioritize relating to others during conflict resolution. Here's why focusing on relating is crucial:

- Empathy and understanding: When you relate to others, you put yourself in their shoes and seek to understand their perspectives and concerns. By practicing empathy and understanding, you can de-escalate conflicts and create an environment where all parties feel heard and respected. This lays the foundation for effective problem-solving.
- Collaboration and teamwork: The goal of conflict resolution should be to find common ground and reach a mutually beneficial solution. When you focus on relating rather than being right, you promote collaboration and teamwork. This approach encourages the sharing of ideas, compromise, and collective decision-making, leading to more effective resolutions.
- Maintaining relationships: Conflict resolution is not just about solving immediate problems but also about preserving relationships for the long term. When you prioritize relating, you prioritize the importance of maintaining positive relationships with your colleagues. This fosters a sense of unity and cooperation within the school community.

By focusing on relating, you can create a more constructive and harmonious environment where conflicts are resolved with empathy, collaboration, and the preservation of relationships. Remember, by practicing empathy and understanding, promoting collaboration and teamwork, and valuing relationships, you can navigate conflicts more effectively and contribute to a positive and supportive school community.

Focus on the Issue, Not on the Individual

When conflict arises, it could be more about the personalities of the individuals than about the actual issues. But when dealing with the issue, rather than individual, what we are saying is that you should focus on the behavior at the root of the conflict and not on the personality of the individuals. For instance, let's say there is a disagreement between a high-agreeableness teacher, Ms. Thompson, and another teacher, Mr. Johnson, regarding the distribution of classroom resources.

1. Establish a neutral and respectful environment: The teacher, Ms. Thompson, initiates a private conversation with Mr. Johnson in a neutral and quiet space. This ensures a conducive environment for open communication and conflict resolution.
2. Active listening and empathy: Ms. Thompson actively listens to Mr. Johnson's concerns, ensuring that he feels heard and understood. She demonstrates empathy towards his perspective, acknowledging that different viewpoints exist.
3. Focus on the common goal: Ms. Thompson emphasizes the shared objective of providing effective learning resources for all students. She highlights the importance of finding a solution that benefits the students rather than dwelling on individual differences.
4. Identify the specific issues: Ms. Thompson encourages both herself and Mr. Johnson to identify and articulate the specific issues causing the conflict. This helps to shift the focus from personal characteristics to the tangible problems that need to be addressed.

5. Separate behavior from personality: Ms. Thompson makes a conscious effort to separate Mr. Johnson's lower agreeableness personality from the current conflict. She avoids attributing the disagreement solely to his personality traits and instead focuses on finding common ground based on professional standards and shared objectives.

6. Collaborative problem-solving: Ms. Thompson engages Mr. Johnson in a collaborative problem-solving process. They brainstorm potential solutions together and explore different perspectives to find a resolution that is fair and addresses the concerns of both parties.

7. Maintain professionalism: Throughout the conversation, Ms. Thompson maintains a professional and respectful tone. She avoids personal attacks or criticism, focusing on constructive communication to navigate the conflict.

Focus on the Future, Not on the Conflict

One of two things results from conflict. Either there is some sort of compromise and a solution to the issue, or maybe there is no resolution and there has to be the "next steps" conversation. Hopefully you reach a compromise more often than not. However, if there needs to be a next step, then that must be addressed without a personality conflict.

For example, in the previous scenario, there should be documented agreements and follow-ups: Once an agreement is reached, Ms. Thompson ensures that it is clearly documented. This helps to avoid future misunderstandings and provides a reference point for both parties. She also follows up with Mr. Johnson to ensure that the agreed-upon solution is implemented effectively.

Remember, as an assertive teacher, you can engage in conflict, but the key is to do it well. It is a skill that needs to be developed. The better we communicate and connect with our colleagues, administrators, and even students, the more successful everyone will be. Make sure you let the other person know that it is not personal and that correcting a problem or issue is all that matters to you. As you can see, conflict or confrontation doesn't need to be avoided, but it does require removing emotions as much as possible and focusing on the issues. While it is human nature to react to situations emotionally, if you follow the steps and strategies that we have just discussed, you can have positive outcomes, even from the tensest of situations. When conflict is seen as potentially improving the status quo or creating healthier relationships, then how can it be viewed as anything but positive?

If Needed, Include a Mediator

In complex or highly charged conflicts, you can seek the assistance of a neutral mediator or a third-party facilitator. This person will provide guidance, structure the conversation, and ensure that all parties have a fair opportunity to express their concerns and work towards a resolution. Mediation can help alleviate some of the pressure on you and create a more balanced environment for conflict resolution. By involving a mediator, you can foster a neutral space where all perspectives are considered and find a mutually agreeable solution.

Overcoming Pressure to be Perfect

I know that as a teacher I – and probably you as well – often find myself feeling the pressure to be perfect. You believe that you must meet the needs and expectations of everyone around you, including students, parents, colleagues, and administrators. The weight of this responsibility can be overwhelming, leading to a sense of burnout and exhaustion.

This constant pursuit of perfection takes a toll on your well-being. You may experience heightened levels of stress, anxiety, and even depression. Doubts may creep into your mind, making you question your abilities and leaving you feeling like you're never doing enough. These negative emotions can diminish your job satisfaction and make you consider leaving the profession altogether.

Moreover, the pressure to be perfect also affects your collaboration with other teachers. You might hesitate to seek help or share your ideas, fearing judgment or criticism. This fear stifles innovation and creativity in the classroom, hindering both your personal growth and the overall progress of your students.

To alleviate this pressure, it is crucial to shift towards a more holistic approach. Instead of fixating on perfectionism, we need to value growth and development. Recognize that making mistakes is an inherent part of the learning process and that teachers, like students, require support and guidance to improve continuously.

Supporting your well-being should be a priority. You deserve access to resources and tools that can help you manage stress and anxiety effectively. Counseling services, mindfulness training, and time management techniques can prove invaluable in this regard. Additionally, fostering a culture of self-care and providing opportunities for teachers to connect and support each other will contribute to a healthier work environment.

Creating a supportive learning environment also plays a significant role in reducing the pressure to be perfect. Emphasize growth and development over perfectionism to encourage your students to take risks and make mistakes. Offer constructive feedback that helps them improve and grow. Cultivating a collaborative culture within your school allows you to share ideas with fellow teachers and support one another's professional growth.

Furthermore, it's essential to prioritize your own professional growth. Seek out opportunities for development, such as attending workshops, conferences, or mentorship programs. By continuously improving your skills and knowledge, you can increase your confidence and effectiveness as a teacher. Recognize and reward your efforts to innovate and enhance your teaching methods, further reinforcing a culture of growth.

Remember, being perfect is an unrealistic and unattainable goal. By embracing a holistic approach that values growth and development, you can relieve yourself of the immense pressure to be flawless. Prioritize your well-being, foster a supportive learning environment, and invest in your professional growth. In doing so, you'll not only become a more effective teacher but also find greater fulfillment and satisfaction in your role.

I would like to leave this section with a wonderful illustration from my old friend, John Smoltz, former pitcher for the Atlanta Braves.

I remember a conversation we had when he shared that his goal was never to win a world series or be a Cy Young Award winner, but that his goal was to give up 200 homeruns.

Some may think that is a not a good goal, but when you really think about it, only a good pitcher is going to be around long enough to give up 200 homeruns. It would take years to give up that many, so a bad pitcher would never last long enough to allow the other teams to score 200 homeruns off of them. And he did even worse than he thought because he actually gave up 288 homeruns! But, he also played for 21 years, won a Cy Young award and a world series, and was a first ballot hall of famer! Much of his success was because of his mindset that he didn't have to be perfect. What if his goal was to be a hall of fame player? Imagine how defeated he would have felt when he gave up that first homerun. He might have even felt a little imposter syndrome. But, with his mindset, after giving up that first homerun, he said, just 199 to go! Think of how much pressure that takes off you when you realize you don't have to be perfect to be great. In fact, mere high achievers tend to do better than their perfectionistic counterparts because they are generally less stressed and are satisfied with a job well done. They don't pick it apart and try to zero in on what could have been better. It is as I like to say, "Sometimes good enough is good enough." So, learn to be comfortable with your best and watch how successful you will become.

Negotiating for Yourself

As I mentioned earlier, many teachers don't like conflict and tend to shy away from it. Much like conflict, many teachers don't like **negotiating** either. And because we don't really like it, we aren't usually very good at it. However, avoiding it can do more harm than good.

So, to become a better negotiator, it's important to recognize your own needs. Take the time to acknowledge that your needs and priorities are just as important as those of others. Reflect on what you require to thrive personally and professionally.

Developing effective negotiation skills can help you set boundaries and manage your workload, leading to a healthier work-life balance. You can advocate for reasonable expectations, manageable work hours, and protected personal time, reducing stress and promoting your overall well-being. You can pursue opportunities for career advancement, such as leadership roles, specialized positions, or professional development programs. Effective negotiation allows you to assert your career goals and enhance your professional growth.

Through negotiation, you can address concerns about your working conditions, such as classroom facilities, safety measures, or administrative policies. By advocating for better working conditions, you contribute to a more conducive and supportive environment for teaching and learning. By developing strong negotiation skills, you can foster collaborative relationships with colleagues, administrators, and parents. Constructive dialogue, finding common ground, and building consensus contribute to productive teamwork and a positive school culture.

So, building your self-confidence is essential. As we mentioned earlier, recognize your strengths, expertise, and contributions as a teacher. Embrace the value you bring to the educational setting. By building confidence, you'll be able to assert your needs and negotiate more effectively.

Just like anything else, it takes practice to get better. So, practice techniques that allow you to express your thoughts, concerns, and needs clearly and respectfully. Utilize confident body language, maintain eye contact, and use assertive language to communicate your requests.

Prepare and plan before entering a negotiation situation. Define your goals and desired outcomes and anticipate potential challenges or objections. Developing strategies to address them will make you feel more confident during the negotiation process.

Active listening is crucial for effective negotiation. Pay attention to the perspectives and concerns of others involved.

By listening actively, you can better understand their viewpoints and find common ground for reaching mutually beneficial solutions.

Aim for win-win outcomes in negotiations. Seek solutions that address your needs while also considering the needs of others involved. Collaborative problem-solving leads to more positive and sustainable agreements.

Take advantage of professional development opportunities that focus on negotiation and communication skills. Attend workshops, conferences, or courses specifically tailored for educators. These can provide valuable training in assertiveness and negotiation techniques.

Find a mentor who can provide guidance and support in developing your negotiation skills. Seek out someone with experience in assertive communication and negotiation. Their insights and advice can help you navigate challenging situations more effectively.

After engaging in negotiation situations, take the time to reflect on the outcomes. Identify what worked well and what could be improved. Learn from each experience and apply that knowledge to future negotiations.

Learning to negotiate effectively will contribute to your overall job satisfaction as a teacher. When you can assert your needs, advocate for yourself, and have a voice in decision-making, you feel valued, respected, and fulfilled in your profession.

 Assertive Toolbox

1. Conflict resolution role-plays: Create scenarios or use real-life examples of conflicts that commonly arise in the classroom. Act out these situations with colleagues or other teachers, taking on different roles and practicing effective conflict resolution techniques. By practicing scenarios, you will feel more comfortable and equipped to engage in conflict in a positive manner.

2. Guided reflection questions: Set aside time for introspection and respond to reflective questions such as "How do I typically handle conflicts in the classroom? What are my

default strategies?" or "What are my strengths as a conflict resolver, and how can I build on them?"

3. Emotional intelligence development: Engage in activities that enhance emotional intelligence, such as mindfulness exercises, self-awareness practices, or emotional regulation techniques. By understanding and managing your own emotions better, you can navigate conflicts more effectively.

Remember, practicing these strategies requires commitment and consistency. By actively engaging in reflection, conflict, and negotiation practices, you can become more adept at handling conflicts and cultivating a positive and supportive teaching environment.

5

Sharing Your Voice

The Power of Assertive Communication in Education

In education, communication serves as the cornerstone of building meaningful connections with your students, colleagues, and parents. As a teacher, your ability to express your thoughts, concerns, and expectations in a clear and assertive manner not only fosters healthy relationships but also creates an optimal learning environment. However, you may have experienced challenges on the path to effective communication, often hindered by two polarizing approaches: aggression and passive-aggression.

Many teachers, especially those who are less experienced, tend to have a more passive communication style. One of the concerns for those looking to become more assertive is with their self-presentation. They worry if presenting more assertive characteristics will make them seem aggressive, which could deter relationship building. It's important to keep in mind that assertiveness is not aggressiveness, so we should take the time and separate these concepts in our mind.

One movie scene that depicts the difference between assertive and aggressive communication is from the film *The Devil Wears Prada* (2006).

In the scene, the character Andy Sachs (played by Anne Hathaway) confronts her boss, Miranda Priestly (played by Meryl Streep), about the way she treats her colleagues. Andy's tone

DOI: 10.4324/9781003453796-5

is assertive and respectful as she expresses her concerns, while Miranda responds in an aggressive and dismissive manner.

Andy begins by stating that she wants to talk to Miranda about something that's been bothering her and acknowledges that Miranda is a successful and accomplished person. She then explains that the way Miranda treats her colleagues is causing them to feel demoralized and discouraged. Andy's body language is open and relaxed, and her tone is calm and measured.

In contrast, Miranda responds in an aggressive manner, interrupting Andy and dismissing her concerns. She uses a sarcastic tone and dismissive body language, such as rolling her eyes and turning away from Andy.

This scene shows the difference between assertive and aggressive communication. Andy is assertive in expressing her concerns, while also being respectful and open to dialogue. Miranda, on the other hand, responds aggressively, dismissing Andy's concerns and using sarcasm to belittle her. This highlights the importance of communication styles in building positive relationships and resolving conflicts.

In this chapter, we will explore the detrimental effects of aggressive and passive-aggressive communication in the educational context and delve into the transformative power of assertiveness. We will examine how aggressive communication, characterized by intimidation and domination, erodes trust, stifles collaboration, and discourages engagement. Similarly, we will uncover the hidden pitfalls of passive-aggressive behavior, which involves indirect expressions of dissatisfaction, manipulation, and avoidance of conflict resolution.

By shifting your focus towards assertive communication, you can learn to convey your thoughts and needs confidently, while also respecting the thoughts and needs of others. Throughout this chapter, we will delve into practical strategies, communication techniques, and role-playing scenarios that empower you to communicate assertively. By embracing assertiveness, you can establish healthy boundaries, foster open dialogue, and create an inclusive and harmonious learning environment for everyone involved.

Four Types of Communication Styles

As a teacher, understanding the four communication styles can be valuable in developing assertiveness and effectively engaging with students, colleagues, and parents. The four communication styles are assertive, aggressive, passive, and passive-aggressive. Let's explore each style and how they relate to becoming a more assertive teacher.

Aggressive communication style: Aggression involves expressing one's needs and opinions forcefully and without regard for others' feelings or perspectives. Aggressive teachers tend to dominate conversations, use intimidating language or body language, and may resort to yelling or belittling students. Adopting an aggressive communication style can create a hostile and fearful learning environment and alienate colleagues. Some examples that may be considered aggressive:

1. Yelling and berating students: A teacher shouting at a student, using demeaning language, or belittling them in front of their peers is aggressive communication. This form of communication undermines the student's self-esteem and creates a hostile learning environment.
2. Threatening disciplinary action: When a teacher threatens severe punishments or consequences without providing constructive feedback or guidance, it can be considered aggressive communication. This approach instills fear rather than promoting positive behavior and learning.
3. Engaging in personal attacks: If a teacher resorts to personal attacks or insults towards students or colleagues, it is a clear example of aggressive communication. This kind of behavior is harmful and can damage relationships and trust within the learning.
4. Responding with anger: When a situation becomes unbearable or reaches a tipping point, anger may be the only way that a teacher can express their frustration and assert their needs.

Passive communication style: Passivity is characterized by a reluctance to express one's needs, opinions, or boundaries. Passive teachers may avoid conflict, fail to assert their authority, and struggle to set clear expectations. They often yield to others' demands or opinions, potentially leading to a lack of discipline or control in the classroom. Here are a few examples:

1. Difficulty expressing needs: A passive teacher may find it challenging to communicate their needs to students, colleagues, or administrators. They might hesitate to ask for assistance, resources, or support when necessary.
2. Avoidance of conflict: Passive communicators often avoid confrontation or conflict. In the classroom, a passive teacher may shy away from addressing challenging situations, such as addressing a difficult student or addressing conflicts between students.
3. Reluctance to share opinions: A passive teacher may hesitate to express their opinions, ideas, or concerns openly. They may stay silent in discussions, even when they have valuable insights to contribute, out of fear of disagreement or criticism.

Passive-aggressive communication style: Passive-aggressive behavior involves expressing dissatisfaction indirectly or subtly. This style of communication can lead to a tense and unhealthy classroom environment, eroding trust, and undermining relationships. Here are some examples of passive aggressive communication:

1. Sarcasm: using a sarcastic tone or comments to express frustration or anger.
2. Backhanded compliments: "You're so lucky to have such an easygoing class. It must be nice to breeze through the curriculum without any behavior issues. Some of us have to work hard to maintain order in our classrooms."
   - This comment implies that the other teacher's success is solely due to having an easier class, subtly

undermining their teaching skills and minimizing their efforts.

3. Silent treatment: refusing to speak or engage with others as a way of expressing anger or frustration.

4. Indirect communication: hinting at a problem or issue rather than directly addressing it, such as saying "I guess some people just don't appreciate all the hard work I put in."

5. Withholding information: refusing to share information or resources as a way of expressing anger or frustration.

Assertive Communication Style: Assertiveness is characterized by clear, direct, and respectful communication. Assertive teachers express their needs, thoughts, and opinions while also considering the needs and perspectives of others. They confidently communicate their expectations and boundaries, actively listen to others, and seek win-win solutions. By adopting an assertive communication style, teachers can establish a positive and balanced classroom environment, where open dialogue, respect, and collaboration flourish. Some examples of assertive communication:

1. Setting clear expectations: As an assertive teacher, you establish clear expectations for behavior, academic performance, and classroom rules. You communicate these expectations to your students at the beginning of the school year and reinforce them consistently throughout. Example: "In this classroom, we treat each other with respect. I expect everyone to listen when others are speaking and to follow the classroom rules we have established."

2. Expressing needs and concerns: You, as an assertive teacher, confidently express your needs, concerns, and expectations to colleagues, administrators, and parents. You advocate for your students and yourself in a respectful and professional manner. Example: "I have noticed that some students are consistently talking during group work, which is disrupting the learning environment.

I would appreciate your support in addressing this issue and reinforcing the importance of focused work."

3. Providing constructive feedback: You, as an assertive teacher, give constructive feedback to your students, offering guidance for improvement while acknowledging their strengths. You focus on the behavior or work, rather than criticizing the individual. Example: "Your essay demonstrates strong analysis and organization. However, I noticed some areas where you could strengthen your argument by providing more evidence. Let's work on incorporating more supporting details in the next assignment."

4. Asserting boundaries: As an assertive teacher, you establish and enforce boundaries with your students, ensuring a respectful and orderly classroom environment. You address disruptive behavior promptly and firmly, while maintaining respect for the student. Example: "I understand that you may have something important to share, but it is important to raise your hand and wait for your turn to speak. Please remember to follow this procedure to maintain a respectful classroom atmosphere."

5. Active listening and open communication: As an assertive teacher, you actively listen to your students, colleagues, and parents, valuing their input and engaging in open and honest communication. You encourage dialogue and create a safe space for discussion.

By adopting an assertive communication style, you can effectively express your expectations, address concerns, provide feedback, and establish a positive and productive learning environment for their students.

Importance of Assertive Communication

Assertive communication enables you to effectively collaborate with parents, colleagues, students, and administrators. By expressing your ideas, concerns, and suggestions in a clear and confident manner, you can actively contribute to discussions, problem-solving, and decision-making processes.

Establishing clear expectations: Assertive communication allows you, as a teacher, to clearly communicate your expectations for behavior, academic performance, and class-room rules. By setting clear boundaries and guidelines, you create a structured learning environment where your students understand what is expected of them.

Maintaining classroom discipline: Your assertiveness helps you effectively manage classroom behavior and maintain discipline. By confidently addressing disruptive behavior or rule violations in a direct and respectful manner, you can establish a positive learning atmosphere and minimize disruptions.

Building positive relationships: Assertive communication fosters positive relationships with all stakeholders. By respectfully expressing your thoughts, needs, and expectations, you establish an atmosphere of mutual respect and trust. This lays the foundation for productive and collaborative partnerships that benefit the students and the educational community.

Effective problem-solving: You are skilled in addressing conflicts or challenges that arise in the classroom. You can openly discuss and negotiate solutions, considering different perspectives and seeking win-win outcomes. By promoting open dialogue, your assertive communication helps resolve issues effectively and promotes a collaborative learning environment.

Advocating for students: Your assertive communication empowers you to advocate for your students' needs, ensuring they receive the necessary support and resources. You can confidently express your concerns, share insights about students' progress, and engage in discussions regarding educational policies or interventions that benefit your students.

Modeling effective communication: You serve as a role model for your students. By demonstrating assertive communication, you teach your students valuable skills in expressing themselves, setting boundaries, and resolving conflicts. Your students observe and learn how to communicate effectively, which can positively influence their interpersonal relationships and future endeavors.

Negotiating and compromising: Your assertive communication skills enable you to negotiate and find compromises when dealing with conflicting perspectives or opinions. By expressing your own needs while respecting the perspectives of others, you can work collaboratively to reach agreements that benefit all parties involved. The goal of assertive negotiation is to find the most effective solution while considering the long-term ramifications.

Overall, your assertive communication skills are vital for you as a teacher to establish a positive and productive learning environment, effectively manage behavior, build relationships, solve problems, advocate for students, and teach valuable communication skills to your students.

Finding Your Voice

Finding your voice is significant for your personal and professional growth, as well as for the learning experiences of your students. By finding your voice, you can bring your true self into the classroom. Embrace your unique personality, teaching style, and beliefs to establish genuine connections with your students. This authenticity cultivates trust, respect, and meaningful relationships, fostering a positive and supportive learning environment.

Discovering your voice empowers you to recognize and embrace your strengths, passions, and values. It provides the confidence needed to take risks, explore innovative approaches, and make decisions that align with your teaching philosophy. This sense of empowerment enhances your overall effectiveness as a teacher and leads to increased job satisfaction.

You become an advocate for change and improvement in education. With confidence, you can question established practices, challenge inequities, and advocate for reforms that benefit your students and colleagues. Finding your voice allows you to actively participate in shaping the educational landscape and make a lasting impact on the lives of your students.

Discovering your voice helps you develop a strong professional identity. Engage in self-reflection, continuous learning, and a deep understanding of your teaching practices. By finding your voice, you gain clarity about your teaching goals, values, and aspirations, leading to ongoing professional growth and development.

You become a leader in your educational community. Your confidence and passion inspire and motivate your colleagues. By sharing your insights, experiences, and expertise, you can influence and contribute to the professional growth of your peers, promoting a collaborative and supportive learning environment.

Finding your voice allows you to align your teaching practice with your values, passions, and teaching philosophy. This alignment brings a sense of personal fulfillment and enhances your overall job satisfaction. When you can authentically express yourself as a teacher, you experience a deeper sense of purpose and joy in your work.

Three Practical Steps to Find Your Voice

Step 1: Reflect on your values and passions Take the time to reflect on what matters most to you as a teacher. Consider your values, teaching philosophy, and the areas that ignite your passion. Identifying these aspects will help you find your authentic voice and give you a sense of purpose in your teaching.

Step 2: Build self-confidence Developing self-confidence is essential in finding your voice. Take small steps to challenge yourself and step out of your comfort zone. Embrace professional development opportunities, seek feedback from colleagues, and celebrate your successes. As your confidence grows, so will your ability to express yourself confidently and assertively.

Step 3: Practice effective communication. Communication skills are vital for finding and expressing your voice as a teacher. Now you may say "I talk in front of an audience of students every day." And yes, that has become comfortable for you. But what I have observed over the years is when teachers must speak in front of adults, they struggle because it is not something they normally do. So, work on adapting your communication style to different audiences. Practice expressing your ideas and opinions with clarity, respect, and empathy. Effective communication will enhance your ability to share your voice with others.

By following these steps, you can unlock your true potential as a teacher, make a positive impact on your students, and contribute to the educational community. Remember, finding your voice is a journey, so embrace the process and embrace the power of your unique voice in education.

Self-talk

Self-talk plays a crucial role in shaping your mindset, confidence, and assertiveness, especially as a teacher. Here are several reasons why self-talk is important for you to be more assertive:

1. Building confidence: By consciously using positive self-talk, you can develop a strong sense of self-confidence. Reinforce your belief in your abilities, talents, and expertise. This confidence will boost your assertiveness when addressing students, parents, or colleagues.
2. Overcoming self-doubt: There may be moments of self-doubt or imposter syndrome when you question your capabilities or feel inadequate. Engage in positive self-talk to counter these negative thoughts. Replace them with affirmations that remind you of your skills, knowledge, and experience. By overcoming self-doubt, you can express your opinions and needs with greater assertiveness.
3. Managing stress and anxiety: Teaching can be demanding and stressful. Use self-talk as a powerful tool to manage stress and anxiety. Employ calming and reassuring

self-talk to reduce your anxiety levels, maintain compos-
ure, and assertively address challenging situations or difficult individuals.

4. Reframing negative experiences: Self-talk allows you
    to reframe negative experiences or setbacks. Instead of
    internalizing criticism or setbacks as personal failures,
    use positive self-talk to view them as opportunities for
    growth and improvement. This mindset shift enables
    you to approach future situations assertively, armed with
    lessons learned from previous experiences.

5. Setting boundaries: Establishing clear boundaries is essen-
    tial for maintaining a positive and productive classroom
    environment. Use self-talk to reinforce your commitment
    to setting and enforcing boundaries. Remind yourself of
    the importance of your role and the impact you can have.
    By doing so, you become more confident in asserting
    your expectations and guidelines to students, parents,
    and colleagues.

6. Handling conflicts: Conflicts may arise within the
    teaching environment. Whether it's disagreements
    with colleagues, challenging behavior from students, or
    conflicts with parents, self-talk can help you approach
    these conflicts assertively. Prepare responses, rehearse
    conversations, and maintain a calm and composed
    demeanor through self-talk. By reinforcing your assert-
    iveness, you can effectively address conflicts and find
    mutually beneficial solutions.

7. Modeling assertiveness for students: As a role model,
    you have a significant influence on your students. Dem-
    onstrate assertiveness through your self-talk and actions.
    Provide students with a positive example to follow. By
    modeling assertiveness, you can help students develop
    their own communication skills and self-confidence.

Remember, by harnessing the power of self-talk, you can
enhance your confidence, handle challenging situations more
effectively, and create a conducive learning environment for
your students.

Power of Listening

Probably the most important part of the communication process is listening. Listening is the cornerstone of effective communication, as it encompasses the art of truly understanding others. It involves more than just hearing words; it involves actively engaging with the speaker's thoughts, emotions, and perspectives. In this section, we will explore why listening is the most important part of communication, examining its impact on understanding, relationship building, problem solving, and conflict resolution. By recognizing the significance of listening, we can elevate our communication skills and foster stronger connections in both personal and professional realms.

When you actively listen to others, you gain a deeper understanding of their concerns, needs, and perspectives. It allows you, as a teacher, to gather valuable information that can inform your responses and decision-making. Actively listening shows a genuine interest in the thoughts and feelings of others, helping you build rapport and trust. This creates a positive and open communication environment where assertive conversations can thrive.

By actively listening, you also demonstrate that you acknowledge and validate the emotions of others. Even in situations where there may be disagreement or conflict, your active listening shows that their feelings are heard and respected. This validation can deescalate tense situations and lay the groundwork for constructive dialogue.

Furthermore, active listening empowers you to respond more effectively to the concerns and needs expressed by others. It enables you to address specific points, ask clarifying questions, and provide relevant and thoughtful responses. This contributes to assertive communication, where your words carry weight and consideration.

Through active listening, you also minimize misunderstandings and misinterpretations of the speaker's message. By fully engaging in the conversation, seeking clarification when necessary, and paraphrasing to confirm your understanding, you ensure clear communication and reduce conflicts. Active listening helps you navigate potential pitfalls and maintain open lines of communication.

By actively listening, you can gather new information, insights, and perspectives. It broadens your knowledge base and promotes personal growth. Active listening also encourages a continuous learning mindset, as you remain open to new ideas and alternative viewpoints.

Here are a few ways listen to relate and understand:

- Get rid of outside distractions: How many times have you been interrupted in a conversation by a phone dinging, ringing, or binging? It is impossible to focus, much less truly relate, if your attention is distracted. Put everything down and shut off all technology. Relax, get comfortable, and focus.
- Don't interrupt: Have you ever had someone try to talk over you? It can be quite frustrating. Until the person has finished speaking, don't talk – even if they say something that causes a reaction in you and you're tempted to inter-rupt. You can always go back to a point and respond later.
- Keep an open mind: Don't judge what they say, just lis-ten. You will have time to process the information and you will get an opportunity to respond. But remember the key is to relate, so keep an open mind to their ideas. They may present valid points that you may not hear if you are busy thinking of your response.
- Use attentive cues: Look the speaker in the eyes. Lean in to show attentiveness. Also, pay attention to the speaker's nonverbal cues. Do their body language and other cues match their words? If it does not match up, then you know the non-verbal cues are speaking the truth. If it does match up then it indicates trust, honesty, and other details.

By incorporating these practices into our conversations, we can transform our listening skills from mere responsiveness to active relating and understanding. This shift allows us to forge stronger connections, resolve conflicts more effectively, and cultivate a culture of open and authentic communication.

Mastering the Art of Active Listening and Assertive Communication

There exists a distinction between mere presence and complete presence. This applies not only to educational settings but also to our daily lives. While we often talk about being in the moment, the truth is that most individuals are fully attentive and present in the current moment only about half of the time. Consequently, we end up missing out on roughly half of our lives, as our focus is diverted elsewhere instead of being fully immersed in the present.

It is crucial to embrace the present moment and be fully present when interacting with teachers, staff, and even students. Countless teachers express their desire for administrators to slow down and genuinely listen to them. Taking an extra moment in the hallway when asking, "How are you?" and truly listening to their response can make a significant difference. By going through the motions or letting our minds wander, we risk overlooking valuable experiences. Leaders, when meeting with teachers or staff, it is important to allocate sufficient time to be completely present with them. Failing to engage fully may inadvertently communicate a lack of value for their time and efforts. This holds true for collaborative planning sessions and team meetings as well. While everyone has busy schedules, it is better to schedule a dedicated time to meet rather than asking someone to "make it quick." And during that designated time, ensure your focus is solely on them. Eliminate distractions such as cell phones or laptops, and maintain direct eye contact and undivided attention. This will make individuals feel more appreciated and enable you to better understand their perspectives, leading to improved decision-making.

Being fully present and practicing active listening in conversations are valuable skills that build trust and foster effective communication. Here are five key principles of active listening:

Pay attention and be present: Dedicate your complete attention to the speaker and be fully present in the moment. Eliminate distractions and focus on their words, body language, and tone of voice. Show genuine interest by maintaining eye contact, nodding, and using nonverbal cues to demonstrate engagement.

Avoid interrupting or jumping to conclusions: Resist the temptation to interrupt or interject your thoughts before the speaker has finished expressing their point. Allow them to convey their thoughts fully and avoid making assumptions or premature judgments. Instead, actively listen and provide space for the speaker to share their perspective.

Reflect and clarify: Engage in reflective listening by paraphrasing and summarizing what the speaker has said. This demonstrates that you are actively processing their words and striving to understand their message. Ask clarifying questions to gain further insight or fill in any gaps in comprehension. This showcases your genuine interest in their thoughts and promotes clear communication.

Empathize and validate: Practice empathy by attempting to understand the speaker's emotions and perspective. Put yourself in their shoes and acknowledge their feelings without passing judgment. Validate their experiences by expressing empathy and understanding. This helps create a supportive and non-judgmental environment, encouraging open and honest communication.

Respond thoughtfully: When it is your turn to respond, do so thoughtfully and constructively. Utilize what you have gathered through active listening to provide a relevant and meaningful response. Avoid immediately shifting the focus to yourself or offering unsolicited advice. Instead, respond with empathy, understanding, and respect for the speaker's viewpoint.

By incorporating these five principles of active listening into your conversations, you can foster stronger connections, promote effective communication, and build trust with others. Last, learn to focus on the present moment, whether you are at school or at home. It is easy to fall into autopilot mode during your daily routines, but it is important to infuse each day with a sense of novelty so that you can genuinely enjoy the present. We are creatures of habit, and often, when caught up in the busyness of our days, we rely on autopilot mode, which prevents us from fully engaging. Giving your full attention demonstrates your value for the people and activities in which you are involved.

Assertive Toolbox

1. Reflective prompts: Use reflective prompts or questions to guide your self-reflection. For example, "How did I handle conflicts or difficult conversations this week? What were the outcomes and how did my communication style contribute to them?" or "In what situations do I find it most challenging to assert myself? What underlying beliefs or fears might be influencing my behavior?"

2. Practice active listening: Actively listen to others without interrupting or jumping to conclusions. Give your full attention to the person speaking, maintain eye contact, and show genuine interest in their perspective. Reflect what you have heard to ensure understanding. By practicing active listening, you can better understand others' viewpoints and respond in an assertive and respectful manner.

3. Communication style assessment: Have teachers take a communication style assessment to understand their dominant communication style. Discuss the results as a group and explore strategies for developing assertiveness while avoiding aggressive or passive behaviors.

6

Establishing Boundaries

It's Okay to Say No!

Last August, I had just finished a PD session in a wonderful town in Colorado and was driving back to the airport. I was searching through the Siri radio and came across a radio personality who was talking about struggling students. Her premise was that teachers want you to be successful and they are willing to do anything to help you succeed. I thought to myself that yes teachers do want students to be successful, but I was concerned with the "they will do anything," part of the speech. She then went on to tell students that they shouldn't be afraid to go the teacher to ask for extra help. I also agree, but it was at this point that she went off the rails. She said that teachers are always available before school, during their "lunch hour" break (her exact words), and that they have office hours built into the schedules after school to meet with students.

As you can imagine, I screamed at the radio at the top of my lungs and wanted to call into the show, but I figured since I was driving, I better not cause a wreck. My first thoughts were what school did she attend, when was the last time she actually set foot in a school, or maybe she was talking about college students, but no, she was talking to students and parents specifically in elementary and middle school. If you have spent one minute in a classroom you know that while teachers do want the best for their students, there is no such thing as an "Hour Lunch Break," and after spending eight hours or more at school, there are no

DOI: 10.4324/9781003453796-6

formal office hours. Yes, teachers will bend over backwards and then some to help students, but when this is the information passed on to parents and students, you can see why teachers feel like there are no boundaries when it comes to school life. The reality is that a teacher's lunch is about 20 minutes, on a good day, but usually spent monitoring students instead of having an actual break. Teachers do not have time built into the day for office hours, although that would be nice! Teachers already spend mornings and afternoons working with students if they need it, mainly because we are made to feel guilty if we aren't all in for the students. However, all in for the students does not include working 10 or more hours a day, spending evenings and weekends on school work, or missing out on personal time because it is an expectation. This is not all in, but it is the recipe for burnout. This is a working life with no boundaries!

However, one of the toughest things for teachers to do is set boundaries. There are many reasons why this is difficult, especially for new teachers. For example, I know some administrators are actually told to get new teachers to agree as much as possible during a job interview since they are more willing to say yes just to get the job. What a horrible first impression of an administration. And no wonder we have nearly 50% attrition in education every five years.

And yes, I think one of the major reasons for teacher burnout is there are almost no boundaries given to teachers. It is like districts, students, and parents think teachers should be accessible 24/7.

Difficulty in Setting Boundaries

As a teacher, you naturally become emotionally invested in your students' well-being and academic success. This emotional attachment can make it challenging to establish boundaries because you may feel guilty or fear that setting limits will negatively impact your relationships with your students.

You face various pressures, including meeting curriculum standards, achieving academic goals, and addressing the needs of diverse students. This pressure can make you hesitant to set boundaries, as you may feel the need to go above and beyond to meet these expectations, even at the expense of your own well-being.

You strive to be seen as a caring and dedicated professional. You may worry that setting boundaries could be interpreted as a lack of commitment or caring, leading to concerns about how you will be perceived by students, parents, colleagues, and administrators.

You have demanding workloads with limited resources and time. You may feel pressured to take on additional responsibilities or work long hours, making it challenging to set boundaries on your time and energy.

Educational systems and school cultures can influence your ability to set boundaries. Some schools may prioritize a culture of overwork or may have systemic expectations that make it difficult for you to establish and maintain boundaries.

I often have teachers tell me they feel teaching is a calling as much as a profession. When you feel this way, you often have a strong sense of personal identity tied to your profession. You may perceive setting boundaries as conflicting with your values of dedication, service, and making a difference in your students' lives. Teachers may feel guilty when prioritizing their own well-being over the needs of their students or colleagues. This guilt can prevent them from establishing boundaries and taking the necessary time for self-care.

I know it seems to go against the very core of teaching to set boundaries and **understand that you have to take care of yourself first to be your best for others**. You have heard the example of putting on your air mask first in an emergency on a plane, so don't be the teacher who passes out because you didn't take care of yourself self first!

Defining Boundaries

Boundaries can be defined as the personal limits and guidelines that you establish to protect your well-being, maintain a healthy work-life balance, and create a conducive learning environment. These boundaries can include time management, workload, communication, personal space, and self-care.

Within the educational context, boundaries play a pivotal role in establishing a structured and respectful teacher-student relationship as well as collegiality among peers and even administration. By clearly defining expectations and guidelines, you create a safe and productive space for learning, helping a school culture to thrive academically and emotionally.

Setting boundaries in terms of classroom behavior, rules, and expectations cultivates discipline among your students. This fosters an environment where effective teaching and learning can take place, allowing you to focus on delivering quality instruction and facilitating meaningful engagement.

Boundaries around time management empower you to allocate your time effectively, prioritize tasks, and avoid excessive workloads. By setting realistic deadlines, planning efficiently, and avoiding time-consuming distractions, you can enhance your productivity and maximize instructional time.

Boundaries are instrumental in achieving a healthy work-life balance. By setting limits on work-related commitments outside of regular hours and prioritizing personal time, you can prevent burnout, nurture your well-being, and maintain a positive outlook, ultimately enhancing your effectiveness in the classroom.

Clarifying your needs and limits is an important first step in setting boundaries. Take the time to reflect on what is reasonable and sustainable for you in terms of time, workload, and personal well-being. Identify your priorities and understand what you need in order to perform your best as a teacher.

When setting boundaries, communicate your expectations and limits in a clear and direct manner. Use assertive language and "I" statements to express your needs and boundaries without blaming or attacking others. Clearly articulate what is acceptable and unacceptable to you, and be confident in expressing your boundaries.

Be firm and consistent with your boundaries. Once you have set them, stick to them. Consistency is key to establishing and maintaining healthy boundaries. Resist the temptation to compromise or bend your boundaries when faced with guilt or pressure. Remember that your well-being is important and deserves to be respected.

Practice active listening when others challenge or push against your boundaries. Seek to understand their perspective while still affirming your own needs and limits. Listen empathetically and engage in constructive dialogue to find common ground or alternative solutions that can meet both parties' needs.

In situations where your boundaries may conflict with the needs of others, be open to offering alternatives or compromises. Explore solutions that can satisfy both parties to the best extent possible. Finding a middle ground can help maintain positive relationships while still honoring your own boundaries.

If your boundaries are repeatedly disregarded or violated, be prepared to enforce consequences. Depending on the situation, this may involve redirecting behavior, having a conversation with the person involved, or involving relevant authorities or supervisors. It's important to uphold the boundaries you have set to maintain their effectiveness.

Seek support and advocate for yourself throughout the process. Reach out to trusted colleagues, mentors, or administrators who can provide guidance and support as you navigate boundary-setting. Share your concerns, seek advice, and ensure that your voice is heard and respected.

Consequences of Neglecting Boundaries

Did you know the world's best athletes set boundaries? In fact, it might be easier to understand if we look at the issues when they don't set boundaries.

1. Decreased performance: Without boundaries, athletes may struggle to prioritize and focus on their training and performance effectively. They may lack a structured routine, leading to inefficient use of time, energy, and resources. This can result in suboptimal performance on the field or court, as they may not be maximizing their physical and mental capabilities.

2. Increased risk of injuries: Failing to set boundaries can lead to overtraining and inadequate rest and recovery. This increases the risk of physical and mental burnout, which in turn raises the likelihood of injuries. Without proper limits on training volume, intensity, and recovery time, athletes are more prone to overexertion, which can have negative consequences for their overall health and well-being.

3. Impaired mental well-being: The pressure and demands placed on elite athletes can take a toll on their mental health. Without boundaries, athletes may struggle to find balance in their lives, resulting in increased stress, anxiety, and emotional exhaustion. Neglecting to establish time for relaxation, personal activities, and family commitments can negatively impact their mental well-being, affecting their performance and overall happiness.

4. Shortened career span: The absence of boundaries can lead to excessive strain and a lack of balance in training. Athletes may push themselves beyond sustainable limits, leading to physical and mental fatigue. This can shorten their competitive lifespan as they may experience burnout or face long-term health consequences. Without a balanced approach and smart choices, they may struggle to sustain their career over the long term.

5. Neglected personal life: Athletes who neglect to set boundaries may find it challenging to nurture relationships, pursue hobbies, and enjoy leisure activities outside of their sport. This can result in a lack of fulfillment and a sense of imbalance in their lives. It's important for athletes to have a well-rounded life beyond their sport to maintain their overall happiness and prevent their entire identity from being solely defined by their athletic pursuits.

Now as a teacher think of how these can affect you as well. You may find yourself constantly emotionally invested in your students' well-being and academic success, often to the point of neglecting your own emotional needs. This emotional toll can lead to heightened stress, fatigue, and a feeling of being emotionally drained, contributing to your dissatisfaction and, eventually, making you consider leaving the profession.

Your failure to set boundaries can blur the lines between your personal and professional life. If you bring work home, respond to emails during personal time, or consistently prioritize work over personal commitments, you may find it difficult to achieve a healthy work-life balance. Over time, this imbalance can erode your job satisfaction and increase the likelihood of you seeking alternative careers or leaving the profession altogether.

Without appropriate boundaries, you may struggle to maintain control and structure within your classroom. This can lead to a loss of confidence in your teaching abilities, diminishing your self-efficacy and overall job satisfaction. Feeling ineffective or unable to manage your classroom effectively can be a demoralizing experience for you, contributing to your decision to quit.

When you continuously neglect your boundaries, you may face heightened levels of stress, dissatisfaction, and frustration. Dealing with constant interruptions, excessive demands, and a lack of personal time or space can erode your job satisfaction and make the teaching profession increasingly challenging to sustain.

While failure to set boundaries is not the sole reason teachers quit, it can certainly be a significant contributing factor. It is crucial for you to recognize the importance of setting and maintaining boundaries to protect your well-being, maintain a healthy work-life balance, and ultimately sustain your passion for teaching. Schools and educational institutions should also provide support and resources to help you develop effective boundary-setting strategies and promote a positive and sustainable teaching environment.

Strategies for Assertive Boundary-setting

One of the reasons I think teachers struggle with setting boundaries is because we are much like a **CEO instead of just a worker**.

In fact, you may be more like a CEO than you think. Having interviewed many CEOs in my career, I have found similarities between them and teachers. For example, you make important decisions that impact the learning environment and the educational outcomes of your students. You have the authority and responsibility to lead and guide your students towards academic success. You must set goals, develop strategies, and make critical decisions to ensure the effective delivery of education.

You both engage in strategic planning to achieve desired outcomes. You must design lesson plans, create curriculum frameworks, and implement instructional strategies to meet the learning objectives of your students. Similarly, CEOs develop long-term strategies, set organizational goals, and plan the direction of their company to achieve success.

You are responsible for managing resources effectively. You must allocate your time, classroom materials, and technology resources efficiently to create a conducive learning environment.

You understand the importance of building and maintaining relationships, much like a CEO. You establish positive relationships with your students, colleagues, and parents to foster a supportive and engaging learning environment.

You constantly face challenges and must possess strong problem-solving skills to deal with them. You encounter diverse student needs, behavioral issues, and curriculum-related challenges, requiring you to find effective solutions to ensure student progress. You must effectively communicate complex concepts, provide feedback, and motivate your students to achieve their full potential.

You understand the importance of continuous learning and professional development. You engage in ongoing training, attend workshops, and pursue advanced degrees to stay updated with the latest educational practices.

You should establish and communicate clear schedules for class periods, meetings, and other school-related activities. By doing so, you ensure that everyone is aware of designated timeframes and can plan accordingly. This includes clearly communicating to parents and guardians the preferred methods and timing of communication. Let them know your availability and response time, so they understand when it is appropriate to reach out and when to expect a response. Establishing these expectations helps create a boundary between your personal time and work responsibilities.

To begin, it is essential for teachers to establish and communicate clear schedules for class periods, meetings, and other school-related activities. By effectively communicating designated timeframes, you ensure that students, colleagues, and administrators are aware of your availability and can plan accordingly. This practice minimizes interruptions and enables you to allocate focused time for specific tasks.

While I hesitate to mention this one, we know the reality is that we do have to work from home sometimes. However, make this more of a rare occurrence than a regular part of your schedule. Create a designated workspace at home where you can focus on your teaching responsibilities. It could be a specific room or area where you set up your teaching materials and resources. When you are in this workspace, it signals that you are in "work mode," and when you leave it, you transition into personal time. This physical separation reinforces the boundary between home and school and keeps every place from blending into your workspace.

Creating routines and consistent procedures for daily tasks can help teachers streamline their time management. Develop structured routines for grading, lesson planning, and administrative tasks, allowing for increased efficiency and reducing disruptions. By following established routines, you can minimize decision fatigue and optimize your workflow.

Recognize when tasks can be delegated to students, teaching assistants, or other staff members. By effectively delegating non-essential tasks, you can free up valuable time and energy to focus on essential teaching responsibilities. This not only lightens your workload but also empowers students and colleagues to take ownership of their learning and contribute to the overall functioning of the educational environment.

Leveraging technology can significantly save time and streamline various aspects of teaching. Assertively adopt and utilize educational apps, grading software, and other digital tools that automate routine tasks and facilitate communication. Familiarize yourself with time-saving features and explore technological resources that align with your teaching style and specific needs.

Advocate for planning and preparation time. Engage in discussions with administrators and participate in decision-making processes to ensure you have sufficient time allocated for these essential tasks rather than them being used for other things such as committees or meetings not related to planning.

Finally, prioritize your own self-care and personal time outside of work hours. Engage in activities that help you relax, recharge, and separate from the demands of teaching.

Setting boundaries is crucial for teachers and CEOs alike. It helps establish clear expectations, maintain focus and productivity, promote work-life balance, create a respectful environment, and prevent burnout. By setting and maintaining these boundaries, both teachers and CEOs can effectively fulfill their roles and create a conducive environment for learning or work.

The Benefits of Embracing Boundaries

So, now that I have convinced you that you are in fact a CEO, you can now prioritize your own self-care and well-being **guilt free**! Now you recognize the importance of taking care of yourself physically, emotionally, and mentally, which allows you to show up as your best self in the classroom. Setting limits on your working hours, managing your workload, and creating space for relaxation and rejuvenation are crucial components of self-care. By practicing self-care, you can experience reduced stress levels, increased job satisfaction, and improved overall mental and emotional health.

Setting boundaries allows you to create a healthy work-life balance. You establish dedicated time for personal pursuits, family, hobbies, and self-care activities, ensuring that your personal life is not overshadowed by your professional commitments. By setting clear boundaries around your working hours and establishing a balance between work and personal life, you can prevent burnout, maintain healthy relationships, and find fulfillment outside the classroom. A well-rounded work-life balance ultimately leads to increased job satisfaction and longevity in the teaching profession. Remember as I often say, if you were not here tomorrow, they would replace you fairly quickly in the classroom, but you are irreplaceable to your family.

By setting limits on your availability, you can focus on meaningful tasks, manage your time efficiently, and allocate resources appropriately. Boundaries provide you with the necessary space for reflection, planning, and professional growth. When you prioritize your own development through boundary setting, you are more likely to engage in ongoing learning, implement innovative teaching strategies, and stay updated with current educational practices. This increased effectiveness positively impacts student outcomes and the overall classroom experience.

Boundaries promote respectful and supportive relationships with your students, colleagues, and parents. By establishing clear expectations, boundaries facilitate effective communication and ensure that everyone's needs and perspectives are considered. Boundaries also foster healthy professional relationships among your colleagues, as they promote collaboration, shared responsibilities, and effective teamwork. Additionally, clearly communicated boundaries with parents help establish mutual respect and understanding, enhancing the overall educational experience.

The Power of No

When we talk about being more assertive, it doesn't mean that you are more aggressive or become less agreeable. Rather it means expressing yourself confidently, directly, and respectfully while respecting the rights and boundaries of others.

You can become comfortable with saying no, without feeling like you are being aggressive or feel guilty because you are letting others down. Simply learn to evaluate requests for involvement in extracurricular activities, committees, or additional projects and prioritize your core responsibilities. Politely decline commitments that do not align with your goals and workload, ensuring that your time and energy are utilized in the most impactful manner.

By prioritizing tasks and focusing on essential responsibilities, you can avoid feeling overwhelmed and ensure that you can devote adequate time and attention to each task. Saying yes to every request or additional commitment, which it seems like we have been conditioned to do, can quickly lead to burnout. By setting boundaries and saying no to tasks or responsibilities that exceed your capacity, you can protect your well-being and maintain a sustainable work-life balance.

Taking on too many responsibilities can stretch you thin and potentially impact the quality of your work. By saying no when necessary, you can ensure that you have enough time and energy to dedicate to each task. This, in turn, leads to better outcomes for your students and overall job satisfaction.

Saying no helps you establish professional boundaries, which is essential for maintaining respect and professionalism. It communicates that your time and expertise are valuable and that you have limits that need to be respected. Setting boundaries allows you to create a positive and balanced work environment.

Remember that you have a personal life outside of your profession. It is important for you to have time for self-care, to pursue hobbies, and to spend quality time with family and friends. Learning to say no allows you to protect your personal well-being and maintain a healthy work-life balance.

So, by learning to say no when necessary, you demonstrate that it is okay to set limits, prioritize self-care, and establish boundaries in various aspects of life. This empowers your students to develop their own healthy boundaries and self-advocacy skills.

Recognize your own limitations, prioritize your well-being, and assertively say no when necessary. By doing so, you can create a healthier and more sustainable professional and personal life, benefiting both yourself and your students in the long run. **Remember that saying no is not a sign of weakness but rather a way to protect your time, energy, and overall effectiveness as an educator.**

 ### Assertiveness Toolbox

1. Identify personal needs and priorities: Take time to reflect on your own needs and priorities as a teacher/

CEO. Do a boundary-setting inventory: Create a list of your current boundaries, both personal and professional. Reflect on whether these boundaries are being respected and whether any adjustments need to be made. Consider areas such as work hours, communication expectations, workload management, and personal time.

2. Define your boundaries: Take time to identify your personal and professional boundaries. Reflect on what is acceptable to you in terms of workload, work hours, communication expectations, and personal space. Be clear about what you are comfortable with and what you need to maintain a healthy work-life balance.

3. Communicate your boundaries: Once you have defined your boundaries, communicate them clearly to your colleagues, students, and administrators. This can be done through conversations, emails, or setting expectations at the beginning of the school year. Clearly express what you are comfortable with and ask others to respect your boundaries.

4. Self-reflection questions: Regularly ask yourself reflective questions such as:

   Are my boundaries being respected and maintained?

   What situations or individuals challenge my boundaries the most, and why?

   How do I feel when my boundaries are compromised, and how can I address those feelings constructively?

   What steps can I take to reinforce and assert my boundaries more effectively?

   How can I communicate my boundaries clearly and assertively to students, colleagues, and parents?

7

Fostering Positively Assertive Relationships with Colleagues and Administrators

Because teachers tend to be empathetic, caring, and affirmational, you value cooperation and strive to maintain good relationships. Collaboration creates a positive and supportive atmosphere where unity and teamwork flourish. By working well together, you promote a sense of harmony that benefits both of you and enhances the overall work environment.

Your effective communication skills, honed by your agreeable nature, play a crucial role in fostering a strong bond and mutual respect between you and your colleagues. You naturally consider each other's perspectives and feelings, which allows for a deeper understanding of each other's ideas and concerns. This empathetic listening and open-mindedness facilitate effective communication, enabling you to communicate with clarity and compassion, leading to fruitful discussions and problem-solving.

Your willingness to collaborate and contribute to shared goals as agreeable teachers further strengthens your working relationship. Engaging in cooperative planning, sharing resources, and supporting each other's initiatives contribute to enhanced teamwork. Leveraging each other's strengths and skills, you both create a more enriching educational experience

DOI: 10.4324/9781003453796-7

for your students, providing them with a supportive and cohesive learning environment.

Your agreeable nature also shines through in the support and encouragement you offer to your colleague. Being supportive and empathetic, you provide emotional support when needed, offering help, encouragement, and praise. This nurturing and motivating atmosphere that you create not only benefits your colleagues but also reduces stress and fosters personal growth. The mutual support you provide contributes to improved job satisfaction for both of you.

However, in any relationship we know there are going to be issues that arise, problems to be solved, miscommunication, differing expectations, and even conflicting personalities that may contribute to strained relationships within the educational setting. So while we desire constant harmony, it is important to know how to handle situations in a positive and productive manner when things aren't going as well as expected.

The Problem with Going Along to Get Along

We often hear the term "go along to get along," but is that always the best advice to take? When I hear terms like these, I can't help but think of the "The Emperor's New Clothes." Do you remember that famous fairy tale by Hans Christian Andersen? It tells the story of an emperor who falls prey to the deception of two swindlers. These swindlers claim to weave a magical fabric that is only visible to those who are intelligent and worthy. The emperor, afraid of appearing foolish or unfit for his position, pretends to see the fabric along with his courtiers.

In reality, there is no fabric at all. The swindlers are merely pretending to weave while the emperor and his courtiers, driven by their pride and fear of judgment, go along with the charade. They are afraid to speak up for fear of appearing foolish: The courtiers were concerned about their own reputation and standing in the eyes of the emperor. They did not want to be seen as unintelligent or unworthy, so they chose to pretend they could see the nonexistent fabric rather than risk being exposed as foolish or unfit for their positions.

We tend to seek social conformity and avoid being the odd one out. The courtiers were influenced by the collective behavior of their peers and felt pressure to align with the consensus. They chose to conform to the false narrative because they believed that others were seeing the fabric and they didn't want to be seen as dissenters.

The emperor held a position of power, and the courtiers were aware that challenging his beliefs or contradicting him could have negative consequences. They may have feared retribution, such as losing their positions, being ridiculed, or facing other forms of punishment. This fear of reprisal stifled their ability to speak up and voice their true observations.

It took the observation of a child to break the spell of deception. The child boldly points out the truth: The emperor is not wearing any clothes. In fact, there are four takeaways from this story that are very fitting for this chapter.

1. The importance of speaking the truth: The child demonstrates the courage to speak the truth despite the fear of going against the crowd or authority. It teaches us that it is essential to have the integrity to speak up when something is wrong or with which we disagree.
2. The danger of groupthink: The story highlights how people can be swayed by the opinions of others and conform to a collective illusion. It reminds us to question and think critically rather than blindly following the crowd, as the truth can sometimes be obscured by popular opinion.
3. The value of perspective: The child was able to see a truth that these adults, who are influenced by their own biases and self-interests, could not. It suggests that sometimes the viewpoints of those with a fresh perspective can bring clarity to a situation.
4. The power of honesty and authenticity: By exposing the truth, the child restores honesty and authenticity to the situation. It emphasizes the importance of being true to oneself and not getting caught up in superficial facades.

The key to speaking up is if you feel that way, others may feel that way as well, but may lack the assertiveness to speak up. I think it is part of being a team player that we too often see it as easier to just go along and then suffer in silence if we disagree. But, if we feel something is wrong or it is an area we have a strong passion for or even an area of expertise, we have to be willing to stand up for what we believe to be true.

As we mentioned earlier, we often have a tendency to avoid conflict, and may find it challenging to express disagreements or differing opinions, even when we have valid concerns or alternative perspectives. This can hinder open and honest discussions within the team, resulting in avoiding necessary conversations, suppressing concerns, or failing to address underlying issues, which can ultimately lead to resentment or unresolved tensions.

I also think as teachers we have been conditioned to have a strong inclination towards seeking consensus and ensuring everyone is on the same page. While consensus is valuable, it can also slow down decision-making processes and inhibit the exploration of innovative ideas, alternative approaches, or in some cases the best solution. Balancing the need for collaboration with timely decision-making is important.

While we don't want to be confrontational or aggressive about every new program or initiative, it is important to see the problem that may arise from always agreeing with crowd. This may be difficult for some of you since we tend to prioritize harmony and avoid conflict. This can make it challenging to be assertive or speak up when necessary. But when you begin to "go to bat" for yourself like you do for your students, that's the assertiveness and passion that will bring about positive change!

Fostering Relationships with Colleagues

While it is true that teachers tend to be high in agreeableness, there are teachers who may be low in agreeableness. This doesn't mean that they aren't caring, empathetic, or non-confrontational, but it can mean they may see things through a slightly different lens. In fact, they may find it easier to set boundaries, focus more on self, identify their strengths, and have other traits that may not come so easy to others.

In fact, being low in agreeableness isn't good or bad, just like being high in agreeableness isn't good or bad, but each has their strengths. But before we learn to appreciate those differences in our colleagues, let's look at some of the positive and negative aspects of low agreeableness individuals. This may help you better understand where they come from and help you to interact with them more effectively.

Positive Traits of Low Agreeableness:

1. Competitiveness: Low agreeableness teachers often possess a competitive nature. This trait drives them to constantly seek improvement, push boundaries, and motivate students to excel academically.
2. Objectivity: These teachers prioritize objectivity and fairness in their interactions. They base their assessments and evaluations on evidence and strive to provide unbiased feedback to students.
3. Self-confidence: They tend to have a strong sense of self-confidence. They believe in their abilities and are unafraid to take risks, which can inspire students to believe in themselves and take on challenges with courage.
4. Independence: They thrive in independent work and decision-making. They have the confidence to take charge and implement their own ideas, leading to a sense of empowerment among students.
5. Results-oriented: These teachers prioritize results and outcomes. They focus on achieving measurable progress and tangible goals, motivating students to strive for success and meet high standards.
6. Individuality: They value individuality and encourage students to express their unique identities and perspectives. They create an environment where diversity and different opinions are respected and celebrated.

Negative Traits of Low Agreeableness:

1. Inflexibility: Teachers with low agreeableness may struggle with being flexible and adapting to changing circumstances. They may resist alternative approaches or ideas, making it challenging to meet the diverse needs of students.
2. Bluntness: These teachers may exhibit bluntness in their communication style, often lacking tact and diplomacy. Their directness can come across as harsh or insensitive, potentially impacting student morale and engagement.
3. Impatience: They may display impatience, expecting immediate progress or results from students. This impatience can create an environment of undue pressure and may discourage students who need additional time or support to grasp concepts.
4. Stubbornness: They may exhibit stubbornness in their beliefs or approaches. They may be resistant to feedback or change, limiting their ability to grow and adapt as educators.
5. Tendency to Dominate: These teachers may have a natural inclination to dominate conversations or classroom dynamics. They may inadvertently silence student voices or discourage open dialogue and collaboration.
6. Difficulty Building Rapport: Their direct and assertive nature can strain relationships with students, colleagues, and parents. Their communication style and lack of empathy may hinder efforts to build rapport and establish positive connections.

It is important to note that the impact of these traits can vary depending on the specific context and the teacher's awareness and ability to manage these traits. It's essential for teachers to self-reflect, be open to feedback, and develop strategies to leverage their positive traits.

Appreciate Differences!

So, recognize and appreciate differences. It's important for you to recognize and appreciate the unique strengths that your colleagues bring to the table, **because regardless of whether or not we have similar personality traits, we all bring different and unique strengths to the educational environment**. We all have different teaching styles, experiences, and expertise that contribute to a diverse and enriching school culture. By valuing these differences, you can foster a more inclusive and supportive school community.

Encourage open and respectful dialogue between yourself and colleagues. Create opportunities for them to share their perspectives, ideas, and concerns. Practice active listening and show empathy to establish mutual understanding. By engaging in meaningful conversations, you can bridge any gaps and build stronger relationships. This is important for building trust with them.

Look for common goals and areas of shared interest with your colleagues. By focusing on shared objectives, such as student success or effective teaching strategies, you can find common ground and build collaborative relationships. Recognize that, despite your differences, you all ultimately want what's best for the students.

Practice active listening when interacting with colleagues. Give them your full attention, maintain eye contact, and show empathy. Avoid interrupting or jumping to conclusions. Demonstrate that you value their perspectives by asking follow-up questions and seeking clarification.

Take the initiative to provide opportunities for collaboration between yourself and colleagues. This could involve team-teaching, sharing resources, or participating in professional development activities together. Collaborative projects allow you to leverage your unique strengths and learn from one another, fostering a sense of unity and shared purpose.

Finally, embrace the diversity of teaching styles and personalities within the school community. Highlight the benefits of having a range of perspectives and approaches, as it contributes to a more comprehensive educational experience for students. By appreciating and celebrating this diversity, you create an environment that values everyone's contributions.

Important Strategies for Interacting with Administrators

I have a saying that I never take criticism from someone who hasn't first valued me or given me positivity. I think it is important that you let your administrators know when they are doing a good job. Praise them for their work, because we all like to be recognized for a job well done. And when they see you are supportive, then they are more likely to be receptive when you come to them with an issue. So here are a few strategies to consider when going to your administration over a question or issue, to give input, or maybe even something of a more serious nature. However, these aren't just strategies to use with your administrators but will work well with colleagues if the need arises as well.

1. Prepare and organize: Before initiating a conversation with the principal, take the time to prepare and organize your thoughts. Clearly identify the purpose of the discussion and gather any relevant data or evidence to support your points. Being well-prepared will increase confidence and help maintain focus during the conversation.
2. Choose the right time and place: Selecting an appropriate time and place for communication is vital. Find a moment when the principal is likely to be available and not overwhelmed with immediate tasks. Select a quiet and private space that promotes open and uninterrupted dialogue.
3. Use active listening: Assertive communication involves active listening. When engaging with your principal, give them your undivided attention, maintain eye contact, and listen attentively to their perspective. This demonstrates respect and enhances the likelihood of reciprocal understanding.
4. Be respectful and professional: Maintaining a respectful and professional tone is essential when communicating with principals. Choose your words carefully, using polite and constructive language. Avoid personal attacks

and instead focus on the issues at hand. Remember, assertiveness does not mean aggression.

5. Use "we" statements: Use "we" statements to indicate that you are on the same team as your principal and are working together to find a solution.

6. Propose solutions: When addressing a concern, offer potential solutions or suggestions. This proactive approach demonstrates your commitment to finding resolutions and contributes to a collaborative atmosphere. Present your ideas with confidence, highlighting how they align with the school's mission and vision.

7. Seek common ground: Identify shared goals or common ground between your perspectives and those of the principal. Emphasize areas where your ideas and their vision align. This approach fosters a sense of collaboration and demonstrates your commitment to the overall success of the school.

8. Stay calm and confident: Maintain a calm and confident demeanor throughout the conversation. Be aware of your body language, maintaining an open posture and avoiding defensive gestures. Projecting confidence will help you convey your message effectively and increase the likelihood of a positive response.

9. Request feedback and follow-up: After expressing your concerns or suggestions, ask for the principal's feedback. Encourage a constructive dialogue by seeking clarification and understanding their perspective. Additionally, propose a plan for follow-up to ensure that the issues discussed are addressed and progress is made.

10. Know your rights: If there is an issue which could have serious ramifications then make sure you understand your rights and responsibilities as a teacher and how they apply to the situation at hand. If needed, seek support from colleagues, mentors, or union representatives if you feel overwhelmed or unsure about how to proceed.

When you engage in open and honest communication with your administrator, you create a collaborative relationship that benefits both teachers and administrators. This open dialogue allows you to seek guidance, share ideas, and discuss concerns with your administrator. By being open, you can access the support and resources you need to excel in your role as an educator.

By cultivating openness and honesty, you foster an environment of trust and respect. By feeling comfortable sharing your thoughts and concerns and by experiencing active listening and support from your administrator, a positive working relationship is established. This foundation of trust enhances your morale, engagement, and overall job satisfaction for you and your colleagues.

Assertiveness Toolbox

1. Practice constructive feedback: When offering feedback to colleagues, be honest yet constructive. Focus on specific behaviors or situations and offer suggestions for improvement. Frame your feedback in a supportive and non-judgmental manner, emphasizing growth and learning rather than criticism.

2. Examine your conflict resolution skills: Consider how you handle conflicts and disagreements. Are you assertive yet respectful, or do you tend to be aggressive or avoidant? Reflect on strategies to improve your conflict resolution skills, such as using "I" statements, finding common ground, and seeking win-win solutions.

3. Emotional intelligence development: Engage in activities or workshops focused on developing emotional intelligence. Enhancing your emotional intelligence can help you better understand and empathize with your colleagues, improving your relationships and communication.

8

Nurturing Assertiveness and Leveraging Strengths

Strategies for Working with Low-agreeableness Students

The cafeteria buzzes with the energy of rowdy students, their voices reverberating off the walls. Food-laden tables are scattered haphazardly, contributing to the chaotic atmosphere. Into this scene strides JOE CLARK, a principal known for his tough and authoritative demeanor. He navigates through the sea of students, his determined gaze fixed on a particular group. This group comprises low agreeableness students notorious for their disruptive behavior, their unity stemming from a shared sense of defiance.

Joe stands before them, his presence commanding yet laced with compassion.

In a soft voice that cuts through the noise, Joe addresses the group.

JOE CLARK (softly)   I understand that some of you may feel unheard and perceive the world as being against you. However, I see potential in each and every one of you. While our experiences may differ, we share common struggles. Let's seek common

   DOI: 10.4324/9781003453796-8

ground and collaborate to build a better
future together.

Surprised glances are exchanged among the students. Something in Joe's approach resonates with them, a genuine attempt
to connect on a deeper level.

DERRICK, a student known for his confrontational nature,
raises an eyebrow and challenges Joe.

> DERRICK (mocking)   What do you know about our struggles,
> huh?

Undeterred, Joe takes a step closer, meeting Derrick's gaze
without flinching.

> JOE CLARK (sincerely)   I may not have lived your exact life, but
> I've faced my fair share of hardships.
> I understand what it's like to confront
> adversity. However, I firmly believe in
> second chances and in the transforma-
> tive power of education. We can work
> together to effect change, but it starts
> with each one of you.

Joe's earnestness catches the students off guard. Some ponder his words in contemplative silence, while others exchange
uncertain glances.

LISA, a student renowned for her rebellious attitude, finds
her voice amidst the charged atmosphere.

> LISA (sincerely)   Do you genuinely think we can make a
> difference?

Joe nods, his eyes brimming with unwavering conviction.

> JOE CLARK (assuredly)   I know we can. Undoubtedly, the
> path won't be easy. We will stumble,
> encounter setbacks, but we will

also celebrate victories. It is time to believe in yourselves and in each other. Together, we can forge a school we can all be proud of.

As Joe's words hang in the air, the once raucous cafeteria falls into a hush. The barriers of the low agreeableness students are temporarily lowered, and an atmosphere of openness takes hold. They begin to share their inner thoughts, concerns, and dreams with Joe and one another, forming connections that were absent before. This scene is from the movie *Lean on Me* (1989). It captures the pivotal moment when Principal Joe Clark, portrayed by Morgan Freeman, addresses a group of low agreeableness students in the cafeteria,

The scene concludes, leaving a glimmer of hope reflected in the eyes of these students. They now realize that someone genuinely believes in their potential and is willing to guide them towards a brighter future.

Learning Is Relationship Centered

Learning is not teacher centered, content centered, or even student centered. And despite what politicians would have us believe, it is not testing centered either. But it is my contention that **learning is "relationship centered."** The relationships formed between students, teachers, and other individuals within the educational community play a crucial role in the learning process and overall educational experience.

But relationships need to have a balance. For example, as teachers we do a great job with the compassion and caring part of relationships, but some may struggle with the boundaries, responsibilities, and consequences part of relationships. To paraphrase an old adage, **rules without compassion cause contempt, but compassion without rules creates chaos**.

As a teacher, if you solely enforce strict rules and disciplinary measures without considering the individual circumstances or emotions of your students, it can create an unwelcoming and oppressive environment. Your students may feel unsupported, misunderstood, or unfairly treated. Remember that a lack of compassion can hinder the teacher-student relationship, making it difficult for your students to thrive academically and emotionally. Here again, I think most teachers do a good job of empathizing and showing compassion to students.

However, you should also be aware that "compassion without rules can cause chaos." While it's important to show compassion, you must establish clear boundaries and expectations. Without guidelines and structure, your students may lack direction or a sense of discipline. This can make classroom management challenging and hinder academic progress due to a lack of accountability or consistency. I believe it is important for students to know you care but also important for them to know you care enough to want their best and for them to be their best. This is accomplished through high expectations, routines, procedures, and yes, even the occasional rules needed to keep chaos out of the classroom.

For instance, I remember walking down the hall one day as a teacher when I heard what could only be described as total chaos coming from the computer lab. I happened to stop and looked in the window to see a teacher sitting at his desk without any control of class and I saw one student holding up his chair as if he were going to strike another student. I knocked on the door as I opened it and asked if everything was okay. This was a new computer teacher who tried to get the students to like him, but he had issues with the discipline side of running a classroom. I won't go into all the details of what transpired with the teacher, but he did receive the help needed to create a better structured and functioning classroom. And if you happen to be a teacher who struggles with the assertive part of running a classroom, hopefully this section will benefit you as we identify some of the reasons you may struggle and strategies to help you become more assertive.

Afterall, to be an effective teacher, it is crucial for you to strike a balance between rules and compassion. You should establish reasonable and well-communicated rules and expectations that promote a positive learning environment. Implement these rules with empathy, understanding, and flexibility, considering the unique circumstances and needs of each student. By combining rules with compassion, you can create a supportive and nurturing environment that fosters both academic growth and emotional well-being for your students.

Potential Challenges with Classroom Management

You may find it challenging to manage your classroom effectively if you lack assertiveness skills. It can also be difficult if you haven't received adequate training in classroom management strategies. Without proper guidance and techniques, navigating the complexities of classroom management can be overwhelming, especially if you are a new teacher.

If you fail to establish consistent expectations for behavior, routines, and academic performance, it can lead to confusion and misbehavior among your students. Inconsistencies in your expectations can undermine your efforts to maintain order and discipline in the classroom. A well-defined structure, routines, and procedures in place can help keep students focused. Students thrive in environments with clear expectations and consistent routines, so establishing a solid classroom structure is crucial.

Struggling with communication skills can make it difficult for you to convey instructions, expectations, or consequences clearly to your students. Poor communication can result in misunderstandings and a lack of engagement, making it challenging to establish effective classroom management. Hopefully Chapter 5 helped you better understand how to communicate in an assertive manner, meaning that you express your thoughts, opinions, needs, and boundaries in a clear, confident, and respectful manner.

You may find it challenging to enforce rules or consequences when students misbehave due to your preference for avoiding conflict and confrontation. It's important to recognize the necessity of addressing misbehavior assertively and implementing appropriate consequences to maintain order in the classroom.

Your inclination to prioritize others' emotions and feelings, including those of your students, can sometimes lead you to prioritize their comfort over adhering to classroom rules or expectations. Remember to strike a balance between empathy and maintaining a structured learning environment.

Inconsistent application of consequences for misbehavior can weaken your classroom management. Students may not take your rules seriously if the consequences are not consistently enforced, undermining your efforts to maintain discipline and order. Or you may tailor consequences based on individual circumstances, attempting to address each student's specific needs. While this may be well-intentioned, it can sometimes result in perceived inconsistency among students.

When conflicts arise in the classroom, your discomfort with conflict may hinder your ability to effectively mediate and resolve them. It's crucial to develop conflict resolution skills to address conflicts promptly and promote a positive classroom atmosphere.

Lack of confidence: You may experience a lack of confidence in your ability to manage a classroom effectively. Building your confidence through professional development, experience, and mentorship will help you establish yourself as a confident and competent leader.

Overly accommodating: Your inclination to be accommodating to student requests and needs might lead to a lack of structure and routine in the classroom. It's important to find a balance between meeting students' needs and maintaining a focused and organized learning environment.

Difficulty setting boundaries: Setting clear boundaries with your students may present a challenge due to your high agreeableness. Recognize the importance of establishing and communicating boundaries effectively to ensure respect, discipline, and a productive learning environment for all.

Remember that recognizing these challenges is the first step towards improving your classroom management skills. Then you can focus on strategies to make your classroom run smoother and more effectively.

Strategies to Become More Assertive in the Classroom

Implementing strategies that empower you to be more assertive in the classroom is vital for effective classroom management, establishing clear boundaries, and cultivating a positive and respectful learning atmosphere. Being assertive enables you to communicate your expectations with confidence and clarity, ensuring that students understand the standards and guidelines of behavior. When behavioral issues arise, your assertiveness allows you to address them promptly and effectively, maintaining a focused and productive learning environment. By being assertive, you create a sense of structure and fairness among your students, fostering a classroom atmosphere where everyone feels respected and valued.

Take the time to reflect on your educational values and goals. Clarify them, making sure they align with your desire to create a positive and effective learning environment. This self-reflection will provide a strong foundation for assertive teaching.

Establish clear boundaries for behavior, respect, and academic expectations in your classroom. Clearly communicate these boundaries to your students and consistently enforce them when necessary. This will help establish a sense of structure and order.

Project assertiveness through your body language. Maintain good posture, maintain direct eye contact with your students, and speak with a firm yet calm tone of voice. Remember, nonverbal cues can enhance your assertiveness.

Practice assertive communication by expressing your expectations, provide constructive feedback, and address misbehavior in an assertive manner. This approach will help you effectively communicate your needs and boundaries in the classroom as well. Use clear and direct language when providing instructions or addressing misbehavior. Be specific about your expectations and avoid using passive or overly accommodating language. Your assertive language will help set clear boundaries and expectations for your students.

Take a proactive approach to classroom management. Implement strategies that create a structured environment, establish routines, and employ proactive behavior management techniques. By preventing issues before they arise, you can maintain control and assertiveness in the classroom.

Recognize and reward positive behavior and achievements. By acknowledging desired behavior, you reinforce it and motivate students to meet expectations. Positive reinforcement can be a powerful tool in maintaining an assertive yet supportive classroom environment.

Develop a confident mindset. Remember, your self-talk is the catalyst for your actions. How you think is how you will act. Cultivate a confident mindset by focusing on your strengths, knowledge, and expertise as an educator. Embrace your authority and expertise and remind yourself of the positive impact you can make in your students' lives.

Low-agreeable Students

As an educator, you encounter a diverse range of student personalities and characteristics within your classroom. Among these, you may come across students who are argumentative, disruptive, disrespectful, or sometimes worse. We often associate such behaviors with the student having issues at home, suffering some kind of trauma, having a bad day, peer influence, struggling academically, or other reasons. However, one reason we rarely discuss is that they may be a low-agreeable student, which presents a unique set of opportunities and challenges for you as an educator. And by the way, research suggests that in any given class as many as 15 to 20% of students may be low in agreeableness. A study by Klimstra et al. (2011) found that 16% of adolescents scored low in agreeableness This means that in a classroom of 30 students you can expect to have approximately 4 to 5 students who are low in agreeableness.

And since it is just part of their personality traits, there are positive aspects and potential difficulties in working with these students. This is not is not an excuse for students to misbehave, but it does allow us the opportunity to understand and help them find solutions to accentuate the positive and change or improve their struggles through strategies that we may not have thought about.

The Good, the Bad, the Opportunities

While low agreeableness students may exhibit challenging behaviors, they also possess positive qualities that teachers can incorporate into the classroom to support their learning and growth. Now how these traits are exhibited in the classroom can be positive or they can be negative. So, in this section we will examine the good, the bad, and the opportunities for growth to help the students be more assertive rather than aggressive or just disagreeable.

Positive aspects of being disagreeable in the classroom:

1. Critical thinking and independent thought: Disagreeable students often possess strong critical thinking skills and are willing to challenge established ideas or norms. They may bring unique perspectives to discussions and encourage deeper analysis of topics. Their independent thinking can lead to innovative solutions and intellectual growth within the classroom.

2. Honesty and authenticity: Disagreeable students tend to prioritize honesty and authenticity over conformity. They are more likely to express their genuine opinions and feelings, which can contribute to open and honest discussions. Their willingness to speak their mind can foster an environment where diverse viewpoints are respected and valued.

3. Constructive debate and intellectual growth: Disagreeable students can stimulate lively debates and discussions. By presenting alternative viewpoints and engaging in intellectual arguments, they push their peers to think critically and consider multiple perspectives. This can enhance students' analytical skills, broaden their understanding, and deepen their learning experiences.

Negative aspects of being disagreeable in the classroom:

1. Disruptive behavior and conflict: Disagreeable students may engage in argumentative or confrontational behavior

that disrupts the classroom environment. Their tendency to disagree for the sake of disagreement can lead to unnecessary conflicts with both peers and teachers. This disrupts the learning process and hinders positive relationships within the classroom.

2. Difficulty in teamwork and collaboration: Disagreeable students may struggle with teamwork and collaboration due to their inclination to prioritize their own opinions over the group's consensus. Their resistance to compromise or consider others' perspectives can hinder effective group work and collaborative learning experiences.

3. Potential for negative impact on classroom dynamics: Disagreeable students may create an atmosphere of tension and negativity within the classroom. Their persistent disagreement or criticism, if not expressed constructively, can discourage participation, stifle creativity, and create an uncomfortable learning environment for their peers.

Opportunities for growth

1. Foster empathy and active listening: Help students understand the importance of empathy and active listening in effective communication. Encourage them to actively listen to others, show genuine interest, and consider different perspectives. By putting themselves in others' shoes, students can develop a greater understanding of how their directness may be perceived and adjust their approach accordingly.

2. Encourage respectful communication: Teach disagreeable students effective communication skills, emphasizing the importance of expressing their opinions respectfully and constructively. Encourage them to listen actively and consider others' perspectives before responding.

3. Foster inclusive discussions: Create an inclusive classroom environment where all students feel comfortable participating. Encourage direct students to be mindful of their tendency to dominate discussions and make

space for quieter or more introverted students to share their thoughts. Implement discussion guidelines or turn-taking strategies to ensure everyone has an opportunity to contribute.

Positive aspects of prioritizing one's own needs:

1. Self-advocacy: Students who prioritize their own needs tend to be assertive and advocate for themselves. This trait can be beneficial in the classroom as it enables students to express their concerns, seek support when needed, and actively engage in their own learning process. By prioritizing their needs, students can take ownership of their education and make choices that contribute to their overall well-being and success.

2. Personal growth and development: Placing importance on one's own needs can lead to self-reflection and personal growth. Students who prioritize themselves may invest time and effort in self-improvement, seeking opportunities to enhance their skills and knowledge. This proactive approach to personal development can positively impact their academic performance and future endeavors.

3. Healthy boundaries: Prioritizing one's own needs involves setting and maintaining healthy boundaries. In the classroom, this trait can help students establish a balance between their academic responsibilities and other aspects of their lives. By recognizing their limits and taking care of their well-being, students can avoid burnout and perform better academically.

Drawbacks of prioritizing one's own needs in the class-room:

1. Lack of empathy: When students prioritize their own needs over others' feelings, they may overlook or disregard the emotions and perspectives of their peers. This can hinder effective collaboration, empathy, and positive

relationships within the classroom. It's important for students to understand and appreciate the feelings and experiences of others to foster a supportive and inclusive learning environment.

2. Disruption of teamwork and cooperation: Classroom activities often require students to work together in groups or teams. If a student consistently prioritizes their own needs without considering the needs of others, it can lead to conflicts, hinder cooperation, and impede the successful completion of group projects. Collaboration and teamwork are essential skills for academic and professional success, so striking a balance between personal needs and collective goals is crucial.

3. Negative impact on classroom dynamics: Students who consistently prioritize their own needs may come across as self-centered or selfish, creating an imbalanced classroom dynamic. This can affect the overall morale and engagement of the class, as it may discourage open communication, trust, and mutual support among students. Collaboration and a sense of community are key to a positive and effective learning environment.

Opportunities for growth:

1. Model and promote self-awareness: Help students develop self-awareness by encouraging reflection on their actions and their impact on others. Provide opportunities for self-assessment and reflection, such as journaling or self-evaluations. By understanding their own needs and motivations, students can develop a better understanding of how to balance their needs with the well-being of others.

2. Foster a sense of community and support: Create a classroom culture that emphasizes support, collaboration, and respect for others. Celebrate and value diversity in opinions, backgrounds, and experiences. Encourage students to support and uplift each other, fostering a positive and inclusive learning environment where everyone's needs are acknowledged and respected.

3. Provide guidance on time management and prioritization: Help students develop effective time management skills to balance their personal needs with their academic responsibilities. Teach them strategies for setting goals, prioritizing tasks, and creating schedules that accommodate both personal needs and classroom commitments. This can help students avoid unnecessary conflicts and reduce the negative impact of solely prioritizing their own needs.

4. Emphasize the value of collective achievements and the benefits of working together towards shared goals. By engaging in collaborative tasks, students can learn to balance their own needs with the needs of the group, fostering cooperation and developing a sense of shared purpose.

By implementing these strategies, students can learn to strike a balance between their own needs and the needs of others. They can develop empathy, effective communication skills, and a sense of collective responsibility, contributing to a positive and collaborative classroom environment.

Positive aspects of being competitive for a student:

1. Motivation and goal-oriented mindset: Competitive students are often highly motivated and driven to achieve their goals. They set high standards for themselves and strive for excellence. This trait can fuel their academic performance and inspire them to consistently put in effort and engage actively in their learning. Their competitiveness can push them to reach their full potential and accomplish outstanding results.

2. Increased engagement and active participation: Competitive students tend to be actively involved in classroom activities, discussions, and competitions. They eagerly participate in class discussions, ask questions, and contribute their ideas. Their competitive nature drives them to seek opportunities to showcase their knowledge and skills, which can enhance the overall

classroom dynamic and encourage intellectual growth among peers.

3. Resilience and perseverance: Competitive individuals often exhibit resilience and the ability to bounce back from setbacks. In a classroom setting, this trait can be beneficial as students encounter challenges and face academic obstacles. Competitive students are more likely to persist in the face of difficulties, maintain a positive attitude, and learn from their mistakes. This resilience helps them develop a growth mindset and embrace a continuous learning approach.

Negative aspects of being competitive in the classroom:

1. Unhealthy comparison and excessive pressure: Intense competitiveness can lead to unhealthy comparison and a constant need to outperform others. Students may feel overwhelmed by the pressure to constantly excel academically, which can have negative effects on their mental well-being and self-esteem. Excessive competition can create a stressful learning environment, where students may resort to unethical practices such as cheating or sabotaging others to gain an advantage.

2. Disruption of collaboration and cooperation: Overly competitive students may prioritize individual success over collaborative efforts. They may be hesitant to share information, ideas, or resources with their peers, fearing that it could compromise their competitive advantage. This behavior hinders collaboration and cooperation, which are essential for fostering a supportive and inclusive learning environment.

3. Negative impact on relationships and teamwork: Extreme competitiveness can strain relationships with peers and create an atmosphere of hostility or resentment. Students may view their classmates as rivals rather than potential collaborators. This negative impact on relationships can impede effective teamwork and hinder the development of essential social and interpersonal skills.

Opportunities for Growth:

1. Provide opportunities for leadership and recognition. Foster leadership skills: Offer students opportunities to take on leadership roles within the classroom. This can involve leading discussions, organizing projects, or mentoring peers. By providing outlets for their competitive drive in a constructive way, students can develop leadership skills and positively influence their peers. Recognize and celebrate diverse strengths: Create a classroom culture that celebrates a range of strengths and achievements. Provide recognition for various forms of success, such as academic accomplishments, creativity, teamwork, and leadership. This helps students see that success is multifaceted and not solely determined by competition.

2. Set challenging goals and benchmarks: Establish high expectations: Set ambitious yet attainable goals for students to strive for. This can include academic targets, skill development, or project outcomes. Clearly communicate the expectations and criteria for success. Recognize progress and achievement: Celebrate students' accomplishments and milestones along the way. Provide regular feedback and acknowledge their efforts and growth. This recognition can fuel their competitive spirit and motivate them to excel further.

3. Engage in external competitions: Encourage students to participate in external academic competitions, science fairs, or other subject-specific contests or other extracurricular activities. This provides them with opportunities to showcase their skills, benchmark their abilities against peers from other schools, and gain valuable experiences.

Helping Them Succeed

Low agreeableness students may encounter various challenges in the classroom, including difficulties in working collaboratively and strained peer relationships. However, these challenges can be transformed into positive outcomes by focusing on the inherent strengths of these students. One such strength is their independence and leadership qualities, which can be harnessed to take on leadership roles within group projects. By allowing them to share their ideas and take initiative, they can guide the group towards success by offering innovative perspectives. Additionally, their task-oriented focus and goal-oriented nature can be leveraged to motivate others and establish high standards for both themselves and their peers. By emphasizing the importance of shared goals, these students can channel their competitive spirit towards collaborative success.

They often prioritize honesty and directness in their communication. By teaching them to express their thoughts and opinions respectfully, they can contribute to open and honest communication that strengthens peer relationships when delivered with empathy and consideration. Their authenticity and individuality can be celebrated, creating a culture of acceptance that inspires others to express their true selves as well. Their tendency to question authority and established norms can be nurtured into critical thinking skills. Encouraging these students to analyze information, consider multiple perspectives, and express their viewpoints constructively can foster innovative thinking and creative problem-solving abilities.

Their heightened sense of fairness and justice can be channeled into advocacy for equality and addressing perceived injustices in the classroom or wider community. By teaching them effective communication and collaboration skills, they can bring about positive change in these areas. To address the lack of empathy and understanding, low agreeableness students can be supported in developing empathy skills through activities and discussions that promote perspective-taking and understanding of others' emotions. Building strong relationships can be facilitated by creating a positive classroom environment that encourages peer interactions, collaborative projects, and team-building activities.

Finally, their reduced cooperation and compromise skills can be improved by teaching them negotiation and collaboration skills. It is essential to help them understand that compromise does not mean sacrificing their individuality but rather finding common ground for collective success. By fostering an appreciation for diverse perspectives and ideas, low-agreeable students can develop a greater willingness to cooperate and find mutually beneficial outcomes.

By understanding and harnessing the positive aspects of what may appear to be poor behavior, you can help these students develop valuable skills, contribute to a positive classroom environment, and maximize their potential for personal and academic growth.

 Assertive Toolbox

1. Practice assertive language: Pay attention to your language and communication style when interacting with students. Use clear and direct language to set expectations, give instructions, and address misbehavior. Practice using "I" statements to express your needs and concerns without becoming overly aggressive or passive.

2. Guided reflection questions: Provide reflective questions for students to ponder, such as "In what situations do you find it most difficult to compromise or cooperate with others? Why?" or "How do you think your behavior affects the dynamics of group work?"

3. Self-assessment: Create a self-assessment tool or checklist that allows you to evaluate your assertiveness in various aspects of classroom management. Assess your ability to set boundaries, communicate expectations, address misbehavior, and maintain control in the classroom. Reflect on areas where you feel confident and areas where you can further develop your assertiveness.

9

Prioritizing Self-care for Lasting Success

In the movie *Eat Pray Love*, Liz, played by Julia Roberts, finds herself surrounded by a chaotic workspace filled with papers and clutter. The toll of her demanding job is evident on her weary face. In this moment, her boss, Josh, known for his unsympathetic and demanding nature, approaches her with yet another task, lacking any personal connection or consideration.

Josh's impersonal tone underscores the constant pressure Liz faces. But as she takes a deep breath, she realizes that she must prioritize her own well-being. With a calm but firm demeanor, Liz gathers the courage to assert herself and address the imbalance in her life.

Acknowledging the importance of the project, Liz expresses her need to take care of herself, admitting that she has been sacrificing her personal life and neglecting her own well-being. Her voice carries a sense of determination and self-awareness that surprises Josh, who is accustomed to her agreeable nature.

Josh, caught off guard by Liz's assertiveness, questions whether she can handle the workload. But Liz responds confidently, assuring him that she is capable while emphasizing the significance of maintaining a healthy work-life balance. She understands that self-care is not only crucial for her own well-being but also enhances her productivity and focus in the long run.

DOI: 10.4324/9781003453796-9

The weight of Liz's assertive response lingers in the air, leaving Josh momentarily speechless. As Liz steps out of the office building, a visible sense of relief washes over her. The decision to prioritize her self-care feels like a burden lifted from her weary shoulders. Embracing her newfound assertiveness, she walks down the bustling city street, aware of the empowering choices she has made for herself.

I think most teachers can see themselves in this scenario because the demands on teachers are never ending. Your plates are always full and there seems to be no end to adding more to them with extra duties, new programs, or curriculum. And our culture as a whole is always quick to judge and question if teachers can handle the job. It creates a vicious cycle where teachers who are caring, empathetic, and kind always go above and beyond but then feel guilty if they don't do even more.

Hopefully throughout these chapters you have connected with the need to be more assertive, to focus more on self, and to realize you don't need to live up to some unrealistic expectations from others or even yourself. But that you in fact must take care of yourself first, before you can be your best for others. So as we wrap up the book, let's reflect on what things you can focus on to help you **be your best with boundaries**! This will not only help you rediscover your passion and help prevent burnout but can help contribute to your overall success in the field of education.

Self-care Is Not Selfish

Your empathy, cooperativeness, and genuine concern for others make you an exceptional educator. You consistently prioritize the needs of your students, colleagues, and even your community above your own well-being. While these qualities make you stand out, they can also present challenges when it comes to taking care of yourself, since you may often find it difficult to set boundaries, say no, and prioritize your own needs, which can lead to neglecting self-care practices. And you can try all the assertive techniques that you want, but if you neglect your self-care then it is hard to bring your best. Just like Liz in *Eat Pray*

Love, **you can't depend on others to force you to self-care. It has to be a decision you make and boundaries that you set for yourself.**

And let's be honest, the relationship between self-care and job satisfaction is a significant one. When you prioritize self-care and actively engage in practices that enhance your well-being, it positively impacts your job satisfaction in several ways:

When you engage in self-care activities, you promote better physical and mental health for yourself. Taking care of your physical well-being through exercise, proper nutrition, and adequate rest helps you maintain energy levels and reduces the risk of burnout. Improving your mental health through stress management techniques and self-reflection enhances your over-all job satisfaction.

You also establish a healthier work-life balance. By setting boundaries and allocating time for personal activities, you can recharge and nurture your personal life outside of work. This balance reduces stress, prevents exhaustion, and allows you to feel fulfilled in both your professional and personal spheres.

Taking care of yourself fosters emotional resilience in you as a teacher. When you prioritize your emotional well-being through activities like mindfulness, seeking support, or engaging in hobbies, you become better equipped to handle the challenges and demands of your profession. This increased resilience contributes to your job satisfaction by reducing feelings of being overwhelmed and improving your coping mechanisms. You are also better able to meet the needs of your students, maintain effective classroom management, and deliver quality instruction. Improved performance and a sense of competence contribute to higher levels of job satisfaction.

A focus on self helps you maintain a sense of fulfillment in your work as a teacher. When you take the time to recharge, pursue personal interests, and foster a positive work-life balance, you experience a greater sense of satisfaction and purpose in your role as an educator.

Overall, self-care and job satisfaction have a reciprocal relationship. Engaging in self-care enhances your job satisfaction, and in turn, higher job satisfaction encourages you to prioritize your self-care. By investing in your well-being, you can experience greater job satisfaction, leading to a more fulfilling and sustainable career in education.

When You Neglect Self

If you recall, in the beginning of the book, I mentioned that teachers are often so other-focused that they usually think of their own well-being last, if at all. And while this may be sustainable for a few months or even a couple of years, it is not sustainable for the long term.

There is increased risk of stress and burnout: You often find it difficult to set boundaries and say no. This tendency can result in taking on excessive workloads and responsibilities, leading to increased stress levels and eventually burnout. Without practicing self-care, you may struggle to effectively manage your workload and maintain a healthy work-life balance.

Your inclination to prioritize the needs of others over your own can lead to neglecting your personal needs. This may involve not getting enough rest, failing to engage in activities that bring you joy and fulfillment, and neglecting self-care practices. Over time, this neglect can lead to physical and mental exhaustion, negatively impacting your overall well-being.

When you consistently prioritize the needs of others over your own, it can significantly impact your job satisfaction. You may start to feel overwhelmed, unappreciated, and lacking fulfillment in your profession. This can result in decreased motivation, reduced engagement, and ultimately lower levels of job satisfaction.

Not prioritizing self-care can strain your relationships with colleagues, friends, and family members. Your difficulty in setting boundaries may lead to increased stress and potential conflicts. This can affect your interpersonal relationships and contribute to feelings of overwhelm and resentment.

Failing to take care of yourself can have a direct impact on your effectiveness as a teacher. Without proper self-care, your energy levels, creativity, and ability to manage classroom dynamics may suffer. This can result in compromised instructional delivery, reduced student engagement, and overall diminished educational outcomes.

Neglecting self-care can take a toll on your physical and emotional health. The increased stress, lack of rest, and disregard for your personal needs can contribute to physical ailments, a weakened immune system, mood disturbances, and even mental health issues such as anxiety and depression.

Finally, without implementing self-care practices, you may experience a decline in resilience. Challenges and setbacks may become harder to bounce back from, and you may find it increasingly difficult to utilize effective coping mechanisms. This can leave you more vulnerable to stress and emotional exhaustion.

Self-care in Action

There are many ways to take care of yourself. We have mentioned some throughout the book such as setting boundaries, learning to articulate your wants and needs, and knowing when to say "No." But here are five simple strategies that are easy to implement to reinforce the importance of putting self-care in action!

Practice stress management techniques: Learn and implement stress management techniques like deep breathing exercises, mindfulness, or yoga. These practices can help reduce stress levels and promote a sense of calm.

Take regular breaks: Throughout the day, take short breaks to recharge and rejuvenate. Step away from your desk, stretch, go for a short walk, or engage in a quick activity that brings you joy.

Engage in hobbies and interests: Dedicate time to activities that you enjoy outside of work. Engaging in hobbies, whether it's reading, painting, playing an instrument, spending time with loved ones, or gardening, can provide a sense of fulfillment and relaxation. And don't be afraid to bring these into the classroom to share your passions with your students.

Unplug from technology: Take regular breaks from technology, especially during non-work hours. Disconnecting from emails and social media allows you to recharge and be present in the moment. This is a great way to set boundaries between work and your personal time.

Finally, have an attitude of gratitude. Set aside dedicated time where you can reflect without distractions. Choose a specific time of the day, such as in the morning or before bed, to establish consistent gratitude practice. I remember as a teacher I would purposely get to school early, so I had time to reflect on the day. It also helped me from getting stressed if traffic was heavier than normal because I wasn't worried about being late. The reflect on the reasons behind your gratitude: After noting what you're grateful for, take a moment to reflect on why you appreciate those things. Consider the positive feelings they evoke, the benefits they bring, or the lessons they teach you. This deeper reflection can enhance your gratitude experience.

To maintain your well-being and maximize your potential, self-care in action is crucial for you as a teacher. You must prioritize your physical, mental, and emotional health through intentional practices and strategies. Start by setting boundaries that establish a healthy work-life balance, ensuring that you have dedicated time for yourself outside of your teaching responsibilities. Engaging in regular exercise and nourishing your body with nutritious meals will provide you with the energy and vitality needed to navigate each day. Don't underestimate the power of restful sleep, as it plays a vital role in rejuvenating your mind and body. Incorporating mindfulness and relaxation techniques, such as deep breathing exercises or meditation, into your daily routine will help you find moments of tranquility and clarity.

Rediscovering Your Purpose and Finding Peace

In the journey of teaching, it's easy to get caught up in the day-to-day challenges and lose sight of your initial motivation for entering the profession, especially since teaching can indeed be a demanding and challenging profession. Teaching can certainly be chaotic at times. The dynamic nature of the classroom, the multitude of responsibilities, and the diverse needs of students can contribute to a sense of chaos in the teaching profession.

You may face challenges such as managing a large number of students, addressing individual learning needs, dealing with behavior issues, meeting deadlines, and adapting to unexpected circumstances.

Additionally, external factors like changes in curriculum, administrative demands, and societal pressures can add to the chaotic nature of teaching. However, despite the chaos, teachers have the opportunity to create structure, foster learning, and make a positive impact on their students' lives. By implementing effective strategies, setting clear expectations, and prioritizing self-care, teachers can navigate the chaos and find a sense of peace and fulfillment in their vital role.

Rediscovering and reconnecting with your "why" is crucial for staying motivated and passionate about teaching. Take some time to reflect on what inspired you to become a teacher in the first place. Was it the desire to make a difference in the lives of young learners? The joy of witnessing a student's "aha" moment? The opportunity to share your knowledge and passion for a subject? Whatever it may be, reconnecting with your why can reignite your sense of purpose. However, to keep from being emotionally exhausted, stressed out, or even burned out, it is important to implement strategies to alleviate these issues.

- Focus on what you can control: Teaching comes with various external factors that are beyond your control. Instead of getting overwhelmed by those factors, focus on what you can control, such as your classroom environment, your teaching strategies, and your own well-being. Shifting your attention to what you can influence can help you feel more empowered and at peace.
- Seek support and connection: Connect with other teachers, either within your school or through professional networks and communities. Sharing experiences, challenges, and strategies with colleagues who understand the teaching profession can provide valuable support and a sense of camaraderie. Additionally, consider reaching out to a mentor or joining support groups

where you can openly discuss your concerns and find encouragement.

- Set realistic expectations: Understand that you cannot do everything perfectly, and it's okay to prioritize and set realistic expectations for yourself. Recognize your limitations and be kind to yourself when things don't go as planned. Setting manageable goals and celebrating small victories can help you maintain a sense of accomplishment and peace.
- Establish work-life balance: Strive to find a balance between your professional and personal life. Set boundaries and allocate time for self-care, hobbies, and spending quality time with loved ones. Engaging in activities outside of teaching that bring you joy and relaxation can rejuvenate your energy and contribute to a greater sense of peace.
- Take breaks and vacations: Use breaks and vacations to recharge and rejuvenate. Step away from work-related tasks and engage in activities that help you relax and unwind. Whether it's traveling, reading, pursuing hobbies, or simply enjoying leisure time, giving yourself permission to take breaks is essential for maintaining your well-being and finding peace.
- Practice self-care: Prioritize your own well-being and practice self-care regularly. Engage in activities that nurture your physical, mental, and emotional health, such as exercising, practicing mindfulness, getting enough sleep, eating well, and engaging in activities that bring you joy and relaxation. Taking care of yourself is crucial for finding peace in the midst of a demanding profession like teaching.

Remember that finding peace is an ongoing process, and it may require different strategies for different individuals. Explore and experiment with different techniques to discover what works best for you. By prioritizing your well-being and implementing self-care practices, you can cultivate a greater sense of peace and fulfillment in your teaching career.

Being More Assertive Can Significantly Contribute to a Successful Career

Being more assertive can bring numerous career benefits for teachers. For one it can help with longevity. Remember the John Smoltz story? His goal wasn't to be perfect, but he knew if he was good enough to have longevity in the league that he might just reach his fullest potential. Remember it takes time to be great and becoming great can open doors and opportunities for you if that is your desire.

Becoming more assertive will help you express their thoughts, ideas, and concerns effectively. Clear and confident communication enhances interactions with colleagues, administrators, parents, and students, leading to stronger professional relationships.

You are better positioned to advocate for their students' needs and rights. They can effectively communicate with parents, administrators, and support services to ensure their students receive necessary resources and support.

As you embrace assertiveness, you open doors to endless opportunities for professional growth and development. By advocating for yourself, you can actively pursue workshops, conferences, and training sessions that align with your career goals. These experiences will fuel your passion for continuous learning, expand your skill set, and keep you at the forefront of educational innovation.

This will also increase your confidence: Picture yourself as a confident teacher, radiating self-assurance and inspiring those around you. Assertiveness boosts your self-confidence and self-esteem, allowing you to step into your role with conviction. With an unwavering belief in your abilities, you will be more inclined to take risks, experiment with new teaching methods, and engage your students in transformative ways. You will be willing to share your voice as the expert you are!

Finally, you are more likely to be recognized for your skills, knowledge, and ability to take initiative. By embracing assertiveness, you can elevate your professional trajectory, create positive change within your educational communities, and open doors to various career growth opportunities This can lead to opportunities for leadership roles such as department head, team leader, curriculum coordinator, or even administrator roles, if that is something you desire.

Assertive Toolbox

1. Journaling: Take time to reflect on your thoughts, feelings, and experiences through journaling. Write about your successes, challenges, and moments of growth. This can help you gain insights, identify patterns, and set intentions for self-improvement.

2. Practice mindfulness: Engage in daily mindfulness exercises such as meditation, deep breathing, or quiet time. Take a few minutes each day to focus on the present moment, letting go of stress and worries.

3. Self-assessment: Regularly assess your own well-being and self-care practices. Ask yourself questions like, "Am I prioritizing my own needs?" and "What areas of self-care do I need to improve?" This self-assessment will help you identify areas that require attention and allow for self-adjustment.

Epilogue

Unleashing Your Greatness to Be Unstoppable

As you reach the final pages of this transformative journey, take a moment to reflect on the incredible growth and empowerment you have experienced as a teacher embracing assertiveness. Throughout this book, we have witnessed the emergence of a powerful force within you, waiting to be unleashed through confident and purposeful action.

Remember, becoming a more assertive teacher is not just about finding your voice; it is about embracing the extraordinary potential that lies within you. You have the remarkable ability to shape young minds, ignite their curiosity, and mold the future generation. By stepping into the role of an unstoppable leader, you not only guide your students but also inspire your colleagues and make a lasting impact on the educational landscape.

As you close this chapter of personal growth, hold onto the understanding that assertiveness is not synonymous with aggression. It is a delicate balance of strength and compassion, setting boundaries while nurturing growth, and advocating for your students' needs while respecting their individuality.

Now is the time, dear teacher, to shed the weight of self-doubt and hesitance. Embrace your unique gifts and talents, and let your voice resound through the corridors of education, leaving a lasting mark on the hearts and minds of those you touch.

DOI: 10.4324/9781003453796-10

In your newfound assertiveness, you will witness the joy of transformation in your students, the satisfaction of seeing your ideas come to life, and the fulfillment of knowing that you have the power to create an inclusive and empowering learning environment.

Remember that challenges may arise on your journey, but your newfound assertiveness will be your guiding light. Trust in your abilities, lean on your strengths, and find solace in the unwavering support of your fellow educators.

You are not just a teacher; you are a difference maker! Your impact extends far beyond the four walls of your classroom, reaching the lives of countless students who will carry memories of you for the rest of their lives.

So, go forth with determination and unwavering belief in your potential. Embrace the art of assertiveness, knowing that you have the capacity to shape the future, inspire change, and leave a lasting legacy as a world-class teacher.

Meet the Authors

Dr. Brad Johnson is one of the most dynamic and engaging speakers in the fields of education and leadership. He has 25 years of experience in the trenches as a teacher and administrator. Dr. Johnson is transforming how teachers lead in the classroom and how administrators lead in the school. He is a servant leader who shares his vast experiences and expertise to help other educators maximize their potential. He is author of many books including *Dear Teacher* (with Hal Bowman), *Principal Bootcamp*, *Putting Teachers First*, and *Learning on Your Feet*. He has travelled the globe speaking and training teachers and educational leaders.

Jeremy Johnson earned a master's degree in industrial/organizational psychology, where his research focused on the application of personality theory in the workplace. His extensive research and knowledge in the field have enabled him to gain a comprehensive understanding of human behavior in professional settings, making him an invaluable asset to any organization. He has 16 years' experience, including a background in administrative processes and procedure development, which has led to the implementation of streamlined workflows and improved efficiency in various projects. His exceptional leadership skills have also enabled him to develop and nurture the next generation of leaders within various organizations.

Bibliography

Booher, D. (2002). *Speak with confidence*. McGraw Hill.

Borgogni, L., Consiglio, C., & Alessandri, G. (2012). Personality and career development: The mediating role of self-esteem. *Journal of Personality and Individual Differences, 53*(6), 779–784.

Burkhart, L., & Knox, M. (2016). The effectiveness of assertiveness training programs on interpersonal relationships: A meta-analytic review. *Journal of Counseling Psychology, 63*(2), 155–161.

Cemaloğlu, N., & Bekleyen, N. (2019). The effect of a professional development program on assertiveness skills of primary school teachers. *Educational Sciences: Theory & Practice, 19*(1), 91–116.

Costa, P. T., Terracciano, A., & McCrae, R. R. (2001). Gender differences in personality traits across cultures: Robust and surprising findings. *Journal of Personality and Social Psychology, 81*(2), 322–331.

Eagly, A. H., & Steffen, V. J. (1986). Gender and aggressive behavior: A meta-analytic review of the social psychological literature. *Psychological Bulletin, 100*(3), 309–330. www.gallup.com/workplace/236561/employees-strengths-outperform-don.aspx

Hoffman, L., & Borders, L. D. (2001). Twenty-five years after the Borman case: A survey of traits, interests, and work values of pre-service teachers. *Journal of Career Assessment, 9*(4), 373–393.

Huang, C. Y., Zhang, H. Y., & Chen, J. F. (2019). The influence of assertiveness on depression and life satisfaction: The mediating effects of self-esteem and stress. *Journal of Health Psychology, 24*(5), 556–567.

Karadağ, E. (2019). The relationship between assertiveness and professional growth in teacher candidates. *Universal Journal of Educational Research, 7*(7A), 51–57.

Klimstra, T. A., Hale, W. W., III, Raaijmakers, Q. A., Branje, S. J., & Meeus, W. H. (2011). Maturation of personality in adolescence. *Journal of Personality and Social Psychology, 100*(3), 501–517.

Kutsyuruba, B., Klinger, D. A., & Hussain, A. (2017). Assertiveness in the classroom: Effects on teacher-student relationships and academic engagement. *Learning Environments Research, 20*(3), 365–383.

Lopez, S. J. (2013, March 28). U.S. teachers love their lives, but struggle in the workplace. *Gallup News*. https://news.gallup.com/poll/161516/teachers-love-lives-struggleworkplace.aspx

O'Connor, J. J., & Robertson, E. F. (2005). *Abraham Wald*. School of Mathematics and Statistics, University of St Andrews.

Poropat, A. E. (2014). A meta-analysis of the five-factor model of personality and academic performance. *Psychological Bulletin, 140*(2), 322–352.

Redmond, C., & DiGennaro, F. D. (2017). The impact of assertiveness on classroom management in urban elementary schools. *Journal of Educational Research and Practice, 7*(2), 135–151.

Vernon, C. (2013). www.weareteachers.com/teach-to-your-strengths/

Weisberg, Y. J., DeYoung, C. G., & Hirsh, J. B. (2011). Gender differences in personality across the ten aspects of the Big Five. *Frontiers in Psychology, 2*, 178.

Wigert, B., & Agrawal, S. (2018). Employee burnout, part 1: The 5 main causes. *Workplace*. www.gallup.com/workplace/237059/employee-burnout-part-main-causes.aspx